50

GARDENING UNDER GLASS

By the same author:

THE COOL GREENHOUSE ALL THE YEAR ROUND
GARDENING WITH CLOCHES
PLANNING YOUR VEGETABLE GARDEN

The Pan American Fl hybrid "Carefree"
geranium. Sow in January or February for
flowering during the summer.

GARDENING UNDER GLASS

*

LOUIS N. & VICTOR L. FLAWN

THE GARDEN BOOK CLUB
121 CHARING CROSS ROAD
LONDON W.C.2

First published 1971
by John Gifford Ltd
125 Charing Cross Road
London W.C.2

All Rights Reserved

SBN 70710141 7

Made and printed in Great Britain by
The Garden City Press Limited
Letchworth, Hertfordshire

CONTENTS

Authors' Note

No great experience is needed to realise how much the gardener is at the mercy of the Clerk of the Weather. Whilst we can put on another garment or seek shelter from inclement weather plants in the open must run the whole gamut of tricks the weather chooses to play.

The advantage that protection affords soon becomes evident and this can be provided in a number of ways, from the simple hand-light to a glasshouse in which appropriate climactic and growing conditions can be maintained and a far wider range of plants successfully grown. Whether it is the humble cloche or the sophisticated greenhouse the degree of protection given will greatly add to the sphere of interest, and open up a fascinating and entirely new outlook on horticulture.

Protective measures will extend the season of growth both in the spring and in the autumn and thus earlier sowing or planting is made possible and crops of flowers, fruit or vegetables can be enjoyed at an early or out of season date. In the autumn the season is lengthened and crops harvested at a later date than would normally be the case. Quality in many instances is greatly improved owing to the controlled conditions and the beauty of many plants enjoyed at a time when, without warmth and coverage, growth would be impossible.

The object of this book is to present to the amateur in one volume a comprehensive guide to the use of glass in the garden. Section 1 deals with cloches, frames and Dutch lights under the heading of Low Coverage, and in Section 2 the work in glass-houses is fully discussed. Cloches have often been referred to as "the poor man's greenhouse" for they undoubtedly represent the cheapest form of protection and are well within the limits of the gardener with only a modest income. Many keen gardeners gradu-

ate from cloches and frame to a glasshouse either heated or unheated, and perhaps ultimately a hot-house or stove section is
added in which to grow the more exotic subjects.

It must not be thought that, having progressed from cloches
and frames to a greenhouse they should be forgotten or discarded.
Cloches, frames and greenhouses all fit into the general scheme
of protected cultivation for, as will be seen in the text of this book,
certain crops are eminently suited to cloche and frame cultivation,
whilst the frame itself is an indispensable adjunct to the greenhouse.

The favourable reception of our previous book *The Cool Greenhouse All the Year Round* lends encouragement to the hope that
this book will prove helpful to those who are just starting with
cloches, frames or a greenhouse or those who want to make the
most of whatever kind of protection they already have. The greenhouse section deals not only with the "cool" house but with the
more ambitious temperate and hot-house which can make a very
considerable call on one's time but also makes an alluring and
absorbing hobby.

The list of plants to grow in the greenhouse is not intended to
be an encyclopaedia of botanical subjects but rather those which,
given the right treatment and conditions, can be grown by the
average keen amateur.

A garden under glass or some glass substitute may well be a possi-
bility of the future. Modern methods of soil-warming, artificial sunlight and automatically controlled watering and ventilation may lead
to completely covered in gardens. The climate and growing conditions of such a garden would be changed and the normal cultivation
of many tender or sub-tropical plants made possible. Nuclear power
producing cheap electricity should eventually make such a garden
under glass no mere fantasy but a practical means of cropping
throughout the year.

We would like to express our thanks to those who have helped
us with helpful suggestions and to those firms who have so kindly
allowed the use of photographs to help illustrate this book.

LOW COVERAGE

I

The Continuous Cloche

History throws very little light on methods of plant protection in the early days of gardening but we do know that during the middle ages the art of gardening was well established in this country and that gardens supplying regular markets had existed in and around London as early as 1345.

The French cloche or bell glass was a very early method of protection and was first mentioned in this country by Parkinson in 1629 in his Paradissi but it was recorded in France some years before this. Parkinson describes the growing of melons under these "great hollow glasses like unto bell heads". It is a matter for conjecture as to whether it was pure chance or experiment that brought the cloche from the alchemists' bench into the garden, but the fact remains that the cloche came into use at a very early date, and in conjunction with the frame and hot-beds formed the basis of a great industry in and around Paris. The French cloche never attained anything like the same popularity in this country as it did in France, although many attempts were made to introduce what was generally known as French gardening. The bell glass had a number of disadvantages, especially in relation to our more humid climate. No means of ventilation was possible other than propping up one side with a block; not a very satisfactory method, and a change in the direction of the wind meant altering the position of the block. They were heavy and awkward to handle and, above all, cropping called for special methods of sowing or planting to fit in with the circular base. In this country however the frame remained for a long time the favourite method of low coverage, although a number of bell jars were to be seen (Fig. 1).

In 1912 the late Major L. H. Chase, M.Inst.C.E., invented and introduced the continuous cloche. This proved to be one of the outstanding innovations in the horticultural world. It had all the advantages of the French cloche and few of the disadvantages. Ample ventilation was provided, it was easily handled and could be moved with little trouble from one crop to another as cropping demanded. Sowing and planting could be carried out in the usual way in continuous rows and so had the great advantage of fitting into the normal scheme of gardening. It was not until 1919 however that any serious attempt to manufacture and market the continuous cloche was possible, owing to the First World War.

The first continuous cloche was of the "Tent" pattern, but this was soon followed by the wider and higher "barn". These soon

Fig. 1. The French Cloche or Bell Jar

became popular with the gardening public and today the continuous cloche can be seen in thousands of gardens up and down the country and in large numbers in many market gardens.

The continuous cloche is essentially a British invention, and the word "cloche" seems to have become anglicised and usually pronounced with a long "O" to distinguish the British pattern from the French bell jar. It seems rather a pity they should have been called cloches at all, as neither the tent or the barn resemble a bell. It is amusing to remember the names they were sometimes given in the early days—"clotches", "clocks", "clochers" or just "those glass things". Some of the older and more conservative gardeners at first rather resented these "new fangled bits of glass" and found other descriptive if not always polite names for them. Nevertheless the value of this simple and inexpensive form of coverage was soon demonstrated and became an essential part of the garden equipment.

Various makes of cloches can be had today and some special merits are claimed for each. The better known makes are described and illustrated in these pages, but the ultimate choice must be left to the prospective purchaser who must decide which make will best suit his horticultural needs and his pockets. He or she may be a little bewildered by the number of different designs offered. If it is a case of protecting a single row of seedlings for a while one of the smaller tent types will serve, but where two or more rows of seedlings are concerned and a longer period of protection needed, something larger such as a barn of some kind will be necessary to ensure greater height and width; but do not overlook the fact that a large cloche will do all and a great deal more than a smaller one and can often prove a more economic proposition. Avoid a cloche that is complicated in design. A well designed cloche will be easy to erect and, when assembled, rigid and capable of standing up against wind. It should be mobile and readily moved without danger of the glass sliding out. Extra ventilation should be provided for in the design.

The original Chase cloche is well known and has now been taken over by Messrs. Expandite Ltd., Retail Div., Bracknell, Berks. The simplest cloche manufactured by this firm is a tent consisting of just two panes of glass 12 in. by 24 in. The glass is held firmly together by means of an inverted V shaped wire upturned at each end on which the glass rests. The whole is held together by means of a spring handle which permits extra ventilation. The width at the base is 12 in. and the height to apex 10 in.

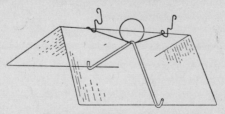

Fig. 2. The Chase Tent cloche

The Low Barn is undoubtedly the most popular of the Chase patterns and there are more Low Barns in use in amateur gardens than any other type of cloche. Four pieces of glass are used; the two roof panes being 12 in. by 24 in. and the sides 6 in. by 24 in.

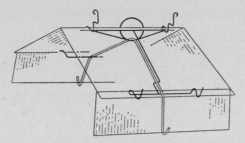

Fig. 3. The Chase Low Barn

When erected it gives a width of 23 in. and it is 24 in. long. The height is 13 in. This allows nearly 4 sq. ft. of coverage. A patent device permits one roof panel to be adjusted for ventilating purposes or to be taken right out if desired without interfering with the rigidity of the cloche in any way.

A larger type of barn is also made and known as the High Barn. The design is the same as the Low Barn except that the sides are 12 in. high. This gives a height of 19 in. to the ridge. Many taller crops can be grown to maturity under these large cloches. A short row of either Low Barns or High Barns with the ends closed does, in fact, become a miniature greenhouse.

A cloche with a flat top is also included in the range of Chase cloches. Three pieces of glass are used each being 12 in. by 18 in. This gives a width of 22 in. It is very easy to erect and is as rigid as the other patterns. This is listed as the "Utility" cloche.

In addition to those mentioned this firm can supply a "Growers Barn". This is similar to the Low Barn but has 9 in. walls. It is designed for the market grower and quoted in quantities likely to be needed by the professional grower.

Messrs. "EFF" Cloches of Binfield, Bracknell, supply a range of reliable cloches. Three types are offered : a tent, a barn and a flat top cloche. The tent pattern has the usual two panes of glass 12 in. by 24 in. held together with a V wire and patent handle, and giving a width of 12 in. Extra ventilation is provided in the design.

The barn or Medium Span as the makers prefer to call it consists of four panes of glass, the roof panes being 12 in. by 24 in. and the sides 6 in. by 24 in. The width is 22 in. and the height 13 in. Ample ventilation is had by means of extensions on the handle.

Two flat top cloches are listed which are of a novel design. Three pieces of glass are used each being 12 in. by 24 in. This is known as the "Low Level" and gives a height of 12 in. A "High Level" can also be had which gives a height of 16 in. A feature of these flat-top cloches is that by means of wire extensions in the design the roof glass can be raised 4 in. to give additional height. The wire frames are plastic coated to protect the edges of the glass.

If a supply of glass is at hand or can conveniently be purchased both of these firms will supply the necessary metal fittings, but it is absolutely essential that the glass should be cut to the exact size, otherwise the cloches will not be rigid and liable to fall apart.

There are also a number of clips to be had for holding the glass together, either in the form of a tent or a barn and when some

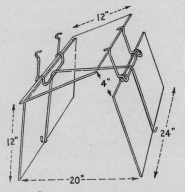

Fig. 4. The Low Level "Eff" cloche

odd glass is available it can be used to advantage. Some of the clips advertised work very well indeed, but some are completely useless. Messrs. Woodman's of Pinner, Middlesex sell a very well designed clip, as also do Messrs. Calvert of Rickmansworth.

Plastic material has been freely used in the garden of late and many makes of plastic cloches will be found in the advertisement pages of the gardening press. A brief word should be said here with regard to the use of plastic materials for cloches for though horticulturally speaking there is no real substitute for glass, it would be unfair to under-estimate the use of plastics in the garden. Most plastic cloches have the merit of being cheaper at the outset than glass cloches, but it must be remembered that the usefulness of plastic material has a short time limit and renewal will be necessary in from one to three years according to the type of plastic.

Plastic cloches are far less weighty than glass ones, but this lightness can be a snare, for unless they are securely anchored they are likely to be blown about. As regards to solar light transmission the difference between plastic and glass is so small that light and temperature during the day will show little difference, provided both are dry, clear and free from abrasions, but plastic structures do seem to lose heat more rapidly than glass during the hours of darkness. Owing to surface tension condensation is inclined to hang about on plastic material instead of quickly forming into droplets and running off as with glass, and a certain amount of badly needed light will be screened off.

Nevertheless plastic has great uses in the garden and where cloches are concerned will make a special appeal to those who are

Fig. 5. The Vitron Cloche

scared of handling glass or nervous of having glass about where young children play.

The type of material will, of course, have a great bearing on the price of these plastic cloches. The "Vitron" cloche manufactured by Messrs. Stanley Smith & Co., Worple Road, Isleworth, Middlesex, is a very good example of a plastic cloche. It is tunnel-shaped and made of stout clear P.V.C. Erection consists of inserting the sheet of P.V.C. into hoops and securing with clips. Extensions of the hoops are pushed well into the ground to give anchorage. Two sizes are available. No. 1 is 18 in. long by 12 in. wide and 10 in. high; No. 2 is 24 in. by 12 in. and 9 in. high.

The Marmex Type "A" is somewhat like a large tent with a flattened top and is adjustable in width. They are unique in that the specially shaped top is perforated to permit ventilation and allow rain to enter. Each cloche is 25 in. long and the plastic

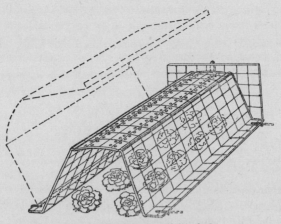

Fig. 6. The Marmax "A" cloche

material used is Claritex—a material claimed to be virtually un-
breakable. No metal fittings are used, the cloche being secured
by pegs. Type "B" is tunnel shaped and mounted on stout wire
hoops. It has a width of 30 in. and is 25 in. long. Again reinforced
Claritex is used. The makers are Messrs. Horticultural Ltd., Goring,
Sussex.

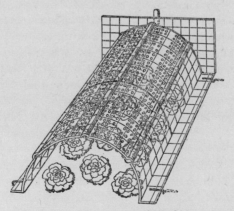

Fig. 7. The Marmax "B" cloche

2

Starting with Cloches

The amateur gardener often starts his venture into protected cultivation with a few cloches. The time available for gardening may
well be limited and cloche or frame work may have to be the sum
of his activities under glass, and he will need to use both to the
best advantage. Many, however, will very soon think in terms of
a greenhouse—heated or unheated—and we therefore devote the
first section of this book to cloches and frames, believing that the
general principles underlying this branch of horticulture will help
towards a better understanding of the greenhouse and its more
exacting demands.

Those starting with cloches for the first time should be well
versed in the functions of the cloche and realise that there is a
right and a wrong way to use them. Cloches fit into the normal
scheme of gardening inasmuch that continuous rows can be made
by butting them end to end and sowing and planting in the usual
way. There is no reason why the odd row of lettuce, strawberries
or what have you should not be given cloche protection but as will
be seen later any haphazard use of the glass can be wasteful and
will not give the greatest return. More labour is called for and the
risk of breakage is incurred if cloches are continually moved from
one end of the garden to the other.

One of the chief functions of the cloche is to extend the season
of growth at both ends of the scale. Thus sowings can be made
at a much earlier date in the spring than would normally be the
case, and the season of cropping extended in the autumn. Protection is given against those killing frosts of spring and the effects
of cold winds minimised. In wet periods the soil is kept drier and
therefore warmer.

Where cloches are used, cropping should be more intensive and
greater demand will be made on the soil. It is better to set aside a

small section of the garden for the cloches so that the special needs of the soil in the way of nutrients and humus replacement can be attended to. It must not be forgotten that under cloches you will be growing the most valued and earliest of your crops and in reserving just that small area special priority can be given in maintaining a high degree of fertility.

The site should be clear of buildings or trees that might unduly shade the area. An open site that gets all the sun that is going is best, and if this is sheltered from the N. and N.E. winds so much the better. While it is true that cloches trap the sunbeams there must be sunbeams to trap. The site must be fertile and well enriched with organic matter if bacteria and other soil organisms are to be supplied with food and energy. Unless these unseen workers in the soil are present at a high level the fullest use of artificial manures cannot be achieved. This is particularly important with cloche cultivation for a soil rich in humus will be more retentive of moisture and the watering problem greatly helped. If there is any underlying pan the site should be double dug. Always choose a site that is well drained and on the heavier clay soils it can be an advantage to grow on a slightly raised bed. Such a bed will be drier and warmer during the winter.

A piece of ground 6 ft. wide will be needed for a single row of barn cloches. This will allow for two positions for the cloches and a pathway. Two positions are needed because more often than not the first crop will be declothed before it has fully matured, and it may be some weeks before the ground can be cleared for the next crop. The cloches can be moved over sideways to the vacant position as soon as the first crop is decloched. By the time the second crop can be decloched the crop on the first position will have been cleared and the cloches moved back again to cover the next crop. In this way the cloches will only have to be moved sideways a matter of some 2 ft. as cropping demands and a profitable and continuous use made of the cloches. The diagram should make this clear (Fig. 8). Where, however, a crop must occupy a position for the whole or greater part of the year a third position must be provided, asparagus or strawberries for example.

This is known as strip cropping and forms a simple rotation keeping the cloches in use throughout the year. Where a crop must occupy the same position for the greater part or more of the year, a third position will be needed. Strawberries or asparagus for instance would need a third position if either were to form part of the rotation. When a greater number of cloches are to be used a double row system will be necessary, requiring a site 12 ft. wide.

The actual crops to be grown must be a matter of personal choice and household needs. A complicated plan is unnecessary but a plan of some kind should be thought out. All that is needed is a succession of crops that will fit into the scheme with relation to times of sowing, cloching and decloching and harvest. This is largely a matter of common sense. Frost-tender plants cannot be decloched until frost danger has passed, nor can sweet corn be sown early in February. There would be no point in sowing lettuce under cloches in June. If the usual vegetable crops are grouped loosely into four groups planning will present little difficulty. The

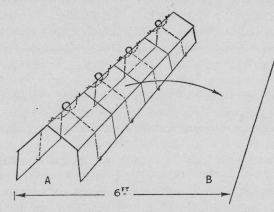

Fig. 8. A strip of ground 6 ft. wide will provide for two positions of the cloches

first group can be those hardy crops that can be sown in the autumn and overwintered or in the very early spring; secondly those frost-tender crops which normally would be sown towards the end of May; thirdly the few crops needing protection throughout the summer and fourthly crops to sow in the open during the summer for late protection as they near maturity. The following table will help you in this matter. See next page.

A three or even four-strip rotation can be carried out if necessary. A three-strip rotation could be :

Strip 1	*Strip 2*	*Strip 3*
Lettuce and Sweet Peas	Marrows	Cucumbers or Melons
(October—Early April)	(April—May)	(June—September)

Group	Crop	Sow or Plant	Decloche	Harvest
1	Cauliflower	Mid-Sept.	Mid-March	Late May—June
	Lettuce	Mid-Oct. or Early Feb.	Early April	April—May
	Broad Beans	Nov.	March	May—June
	Peas	Nov.	March	Mid-May
	Carrots	Late Jan.	Early April	May
	Onions	Late Jan.	March	September
	Spinach	Late Jan.	Late March	Late April
	Turnips	Late Feb.	April	Mid-May
	Beetroot	Late Feb.	April	Mid-May
2	Dwarf Beans	Late March	Mid-May	June
	Runner Beans	Mid-April	Late May	Mid-July
	Marrows	Mid-April	Late May	Early July
	Sweet Corn	Mid-April	Late May	July
	Tomatoes	Mid-April	Late May	Mid-July
3	Cucumbers		Covered throughout Summer	Late July
	Melons			August
	Aubergine	Early June		August
	Capsicum			August
4	Dwarf Beans	Mid-July	These crops should be sown in the open and cloched as they near maturity.	
	Carrots			
	Peas			
	Lettuce	Mid-Aug.		
	Endive	Mid-Aug.		
	Spinach	Sept.		
	Salad Onions	Mid-Aug.		

The dates suggested are for the earliest sowings and planting in the Home Counties. In the North and more exposed areas spring sowings may have to be deferred for two or three weeks while in the S.W. sowings may sometimes be advanced.

Where a number of cloches are in use and cropping on a larger scale the cloche rows should be in pairs and each strip would need to be 12 ft. wide.

Let us imagine a very simple rotation. Having prepared the site lettuce may be sown on position 1. This will be done in mid-October to provide heads during April. They will need coverage throughout the winter. At the end of March or in very early April the crop can be decloched and the cloches moved over to the vacant position alongside. Here, while the lettuce mature and are finally cut, dwarf beans can be sown, for these are rather more hardy than the runners, but they will need cloching until towards the end of May or when all fear of frosts have passed. By this time the lettuce will have been cleared and the site prepared for another crop. We must look to group 3 for this and cucumbers may be the choice. The cucumber plants can be planted out in early June and the cloches moved over to them where they must stay for the rest of the summer.

Meanwhile the dwarf beans will have matured on position 2 which, by the middle of July, will be ready for yet another crop. This can be one from the fourth group sown in the open. Towards the end of September the cloche will no longer be needed on the cucumbers and moved over to give a short period of protection to whatever crop has been sown. It might well be a sowing of lettuce made in early August to provide late cutting. Under cloches these would be available well into the autumn. Fig. 9 will show at a glance the sequence of movements.

It will be seen that with little trouble the cloches can be kept busy throughout the year. Many other combinations of cropping will suggest themselves for the possibilities are immense. Do not be tempted to use the cloches for just one favourite crop but always arrange for a convenient crop to precede and one or more to follow rather than letting the cloches stand idle with the risk of being broken or parts lost.

The advantages of inter-cropping must not be overlooked. Examples are carrots or salad onions between rows of lettuce; a row of cos lettuce between two rows of cabbage lettuce. Radish seed can be mixed in with turnips or beetroot; dwarf beans go very well between sweet corn. Inter-cropping must never be overdone, but must always be such that it does not interfere with the main crop.

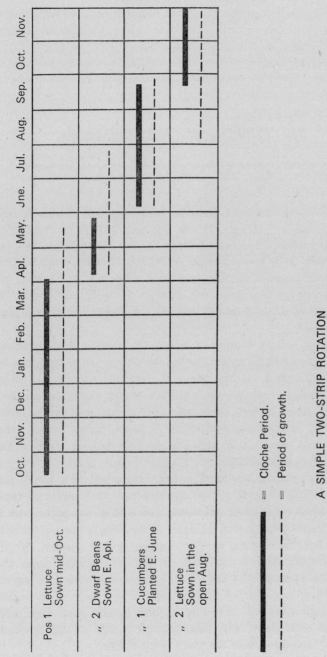

Fig. 9. *A simple two strip rotation showing periods of coverage and total periods of growth*

3

The Technique of Cloche Cultivation

THE SOIL

With or without cloches success in gardening will depend largely on the thorough cultivation of the soil and there is no real difference in preparing the ground for a cloche garden than for any other garden. It is just a matter of degree. Fertility must be built up and maintained if consistently good crops are to be had; but where cloches are concerned the necessity for good cultivation, the replacement of organic matter and the intelligent use of lime must be emphasised.

The use of animal manure or well made compost is an outstanding factor in maintaining fertility but the scarcity of animal manure presents a problem in these days of motor transport, and every scrap of suitable vegetable waste should be composted and returned to the soil when broken down. Additional supplies can be made available by composting a quantity of straw, fallen leaves, green bracken, peat, etc. but if you can possibly buy in some strawy manure do not fail to do so.

Soils vary considerably from a light sandy soil to a heavy clay and from chalk to peat; all vary in structure and degree of fertility. One must be content and make the best of whatever type of soil one has, but much can be done to improve a poor or difficult soil. Do not think that by just putting a few cloches on the garden without paying attention to the soil beneath them that miraculous results will be had. Such an idea is as foolish as expecting a baby to grow into a healthy child if it is only given shelter. Cloches can only, by affording shelter, create such favourable conditions that plants can take full advantage of the available food : they can never take the place of plant food.

On a small area digging will not present any great difficulty but it should be well done. A good spade with a sharp clean blade is needed and thrust down to its limit and any underlying pan loosened up with a fork. A stainless spade is a good investment where funds permit, or a convenient birthday may offer an opportunity to acquire one. Digging, double digging, ridging and finally breaking down to seed-bed tilth have all been effectively dealt with in many gardening books and we feel that the space available here can be better used in describing the best methods of handling the cloches.

SETTING OUT THE CLOCHES

Care is needed in setting out the cloches. First see that after erecting them the glass is evenly placed so that they will butt closely together. Always use a taut line and set the cloches against it. A row that has several bends in it will not only look untidy and slipshod but in many cases the drills in which the seed is sown will be closer than would normally be the case, and unless both drills and cloches are parallel there will be a danger of plants in the outer drills growing against the glass or just outside.

Any stones lying on the soil where the sides of the cloches will stand should be drawn off, for if the cloche is put down clumsily and hits a stone a small crack may be started which during a frosty spell may extend right across the pane. Frost is often blamed for a crack brought about in this way.

As to whether rows of cloches should run from north to south or from east to west may have to be determined by the general layout of the land but generally speaking a N.—S. direction will give a more even distribution of light.

WARMING THE SOIL

During the colder and wetter months it is important to have the cloches in position a week or even ten days before sowing is due. This pre-sowing coverage will not only tend to warm up and dry the surface of the soil and ensure quick and even germination, but the drying effect will make the final breaking down to the required tilth possible at a time when otherwise it would be out of the question. This is a point that should be borne in mind when making those early sowings in January and February for just those few degrees of warmth and the drier top inch where the seeds will rest can make a vast difference in germination.

CLOSING THE ENDS OF THE ROWS

Always—summer and winter—keep the ends of the rows closed with glass, polythene sheets, asbestos-cement sheets or wood. Whatever is used should be securely fixed. This can be easily done by pushing a cane or thick wire close to the outside of the glass or whatever is used and tying the cane to the handle of the first cloche. The reason for closing the ends is obvious—it prevents the row of cloches becoming a wind tunnel for no seedling will be happy under such conditions; it keeps out cats and birds and prevents gales of wind lifting the cloches. Closing the ends also helps to keep the warmth in. Open ends to the plants is analogous to the gardener having to live in a house where the front and back door is always open (Fig. 10).

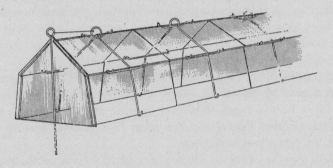

Fig. 10. The ends of the row should be closed. A wire stake or cane pushed in close to the end will hold the end piece

WEEDING AND CULTIVATING

Sooner or later it will be necessary to get at the crop to cultivate. Seedlings will have to be thinned and perhaps syringed or dusted against pests or disease. Never, never remove a cloche here and there and put it down anywhere nearby or just behind. A step one way or another by you or a companion can be disastrous and breakages or even accidents can happen so quickly.

Tending the crops will necessitate either removing a roof panel or moving a cloche. Usually it will be a case of moving a cloche, and the best method is to remove one or two cloches from one end of the row and place them in a safe place at the other end. In moving the first one or two cloches an area large enough to work on will be exposed, and having done what may be necessary the next two are moved up to take the place of the first two, thus exposing another small area of ground. This goes on progressively until the end of the row is reached, where the first two cloches will be found to again complete the recovering. The end glasses are then replaced. During a hard spell when the bottom edges of the glass may become frozen into the ground do not attempt to move the cloches but wait until the ground thaws out.

SPACING THE CLOCHES

As the weather becomes warmer it is sometimes advisable, with certain crops, to slightly space the cloches to admit more air and to prevent too high a temperature or to facilitate pollination. Do not remove the end pieces or give too great a gap between the cloches where birds can be a nuisance as with strawberries.

SHADING

During the sunnier months some light shading should be given. Heavy shading is neither necessary or desirable but give just sufficient to break up the direct rays of the sun. This will help to prevent scorching and will keep the temperature within bounds. A light flecking over the roof glass with lime-wash applied with a whitewash brush will do the trick quite well. The first hard rain will wash a great deal off but this will be all to the good for the time being, and on the return of sunny weather the shading can be renewed in a few minutes.

RAISING THE CLOCHES

In spite of any planned rotation it is not always possible to decloche a row of plants at exactly the time planned, and a little latitude must be allowed in case of unsuitable weather conditions at that particular time. Good growing conditions too may have previously brought on quicker growth than usual and the growing point may be in danger of being distorted. It would be folly to decloche the tomato plants during the third week in May if further frosts were forecast or a cold wind blowing at the time. The only safe course would be to raise the cloches in some way, if only by an inch or two or to use higher ones. Usually it will be a case of raising the cloches in some way. If a number of bricks are available they can be used as shown in Fig. 11. Pieces of wood or small flower pots will do for a few days.

One firm will supply extra wires and glass on which to raise the cloches and they can be had from any garden centre. This arrange-

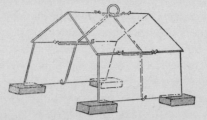

Fig. 11. The cloches can be raised on bricks to give a little extra height

ment will permit the cloches to be raised some 12 in. The fact that a gap will be left along the bottom if bricks or pots are used will not matter at this time of the year (**Fig. 12**).

WRAPPING

Another method to adopt if tall growing plants such as early tomatoes become too tall is to decloche and stand the cloches on end on the windward side of the plants. This will protect the plants on three sides and if any spare cloches are available two placed on end will completely "wrap" the plants. In the likelihood of frost, mats can be laid over the top at night but must be removed the next morning.

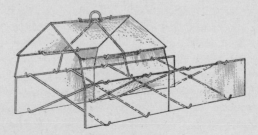

Fig. 12. A method of raising cloches. Extra sheets of glass form the sides and are held by diagonal wires. The cloches stand on short extensions of the wires

AS A HANDLIGHT

Although normally cloches should be used in a continuous row there is no reason why just one or two should not be used as a handlight when the need arises. With the ends cloched a perfect handlight is had. Where small sowings of brassicas for planting out later are needed a single cloche can be very useful. Cuttings can be struck in this way or separate plants such as Helliborus niger (the Christmas Rose) can be given protection. Certain valued alpines will be safer if given coverage and a single cloche is ideal for this purpose. The cloche will serve as an umbrella and in this case we can break the rule and leave the ends open.

STACKING

It does sometimes happen that at least some cloches may have to go out of use during the summer. Any not in use should be carefully stacked in a safe place. There is no need, with glass cloches, to take them apart but simply turn them on end and fit them closely together so that they nest one within the other. It is surprising how many cloches can be stacked on a small area in this way. Never leave the cloches lying about where they were last used. They are almost certain to become broken and metal parts lost.

Before stacking cover the ground with black polythene to prevent weeds growing up between the cloches. Weeds, especially bindweed, can be a great nuisance if allowed to become entangled with the wire frames.

CLEANLINESS

The glass must be kept clean if maximum light is to be admitted. Glass, or any other material that is obscured by dirt, algae or chemical deposit will screen off much of the available light. During autumn and winter months it is more essential than ever that the plants should have all the light that is going and before the cloches are used they should be thoroughly washed.

There is no need to take the cloches apart to wash them; it is easier in fact to wash them while they are assembled. One way is to stand the cloches on a sack or two and with plenty of water at hand the cleaning will not be difficult. It can be a messy job and one for rubber boots, but a job that is well worth while. A soft spoke brush is a good tool to use as it can be pushed in under the wires.

Spoke brushes are not easy to come by these days but a white-wash brush will do the job equally well. Any of the household detergents will remove the dirt and stains.

Where large numbers are concerned a temporary tank can be made with stout polythene. It should be large enough to hold a considerable quantity of water and the cloches stood in this for cleaning and rinsing. If the "tank" is laid on level ground or on a cemented area a little ingenuity will soon find a way to support the sides and corners. Put a few tiles on the bottom or better still a rubber mat to prevent the glass cutting the polythene.

WATERING

A very natural question from the beginner is "How do I water the plants under cloches?" A great deal of needless anxiety is felt in this matter of watering. The fact is that many plants are drowned long before they have a chance of dying of old age and one of the features of cloche cultivation is that excessive rain is kept off both plants and the soil immediately round the plants. As no direct rain will fall on the protected area the soil never packs down or pans but the surface retains the fine tilth given when cultivation was first completed. In other words the surface retains that friable condition that otherwise must be maintained by hoeing. A friable surface makes it possible for air to penetrate to the roots at all times; the soil is warmer and healthy growth can continue unchecked. Notice the difference in the appearance of soil that has (a) been under cloches for a few weeks and (b) that which has been exposed to rain over the same period.

The answer to the question "Do I have to move the cloches when the plants want watering?" is "No". If the cloches are taken off and water given the soil will soon pack down and the useful mulch lost; hoeing must then be carried out to loosen up the surface again. The whole vexed question of watering is, as we have already said, closely bound up with the proper preparation of the soil. If the soil is well charged with humus it will absorb and hold the moisture. When humus is lacking the soil will quickly dry out. Providing the soil is well prepared a reserve of moisture will be held and rain falling on the cloches will run down on either side and seep in under the glass. During a normal season enough natural rain will fall over and alongside the cloches to enable the reserve to be maintained and supply the plants with their needs. The principal movement will be downwards but when the soil contains plenty of humus the lateral movement will be accelerated from either side. Also it should be remembered that roots not only grow downwards but sideways.

During periods of drought artificial watering may be necessary. The same principles will apply and water should be given by pouring it over the cloches. It must be given in generous quantities so that the depleted reserves are built up again. On commercial holdings a system of overhead irrigation is used and directed over the cloches.

The condition of the soil should be the guiding factor when deciding if water is needed. Do not be deceived in thinking that, because the surface looks dry and dusty, water is needed. Scratch down under the surface to the extent of an inch or so when you will often find that the soil is quite moist. If on scratching a little deeper still no moisture is found then water should be given. It is wrong to gauge the need for water by the look of the plants. Water should be given before the plants wilt and if you can gauge this there will be no wilting or check in growth.

A single row or two of cloches can be watered by pouring the water over the cloches from a large can or hose. Liberal quantities will be needed so that the ground alongside is well soddened. A shallow drill drawn on either side will help to keep the water where it is needed most. A labour-saving device can be made by fixing a rose or adjustable sprinkler to the hose and tied to a stout stake or the handle of a fork and moved progressively along the rows so that the jet plays over the cloches (Fig. 13). Another method is

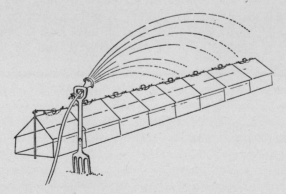

Fig. 13. Hose with sprinkler attached and tied to the handle of a fork or stout cane will save much trouble when water is needed. The spray should be directed over the cloches and moved along the row as required

to run perforated polythene tubing along each side. The tubing
is perforated at 12 in. to 15 in. intervals and can be left running
for some hours to give a thorough watering by means of a low
pressure. Meanwhile other work can be undertaken.

In thinking in terms of watering it must be remembered that
moisture movement through the soil is a slow process but with an
average cloche width of 22 in. moisture has only 11 in. to travel
from either side. In many cases there will be two or more rows of
plants under the cloches and two rows at least will be even nearer
the source of supply. Remember too that the root systems of plants
are much more extensive than is generally thought, and lateral
roots soon meet up with the incoming moisture. In the case of two
rows of lettuce the root system may extend well outside the
cloches.

PATHS

It may sound wasteful to devote space to paths but this becomes
necessary in many cases. If the path is too narrow there can be a
risk of kicking or treading on a cloche and room is needed in which
to turn or place a basket. Pathways should never be trodden down
to road hardness and an occasional forking through will be all to
the good. Rain or artificial watering will leave pools on a hard
surface which, instead of being absorbed by the soil, will evaporate
and be wasted. On a sloping site water will quickly run off unless
the pathway is loosened.

During winter straw can be placed along the pathways between
rows of cloches. This will make for easier working and help to
keep the soil warm near the cloches. A little thrown up over the
cloches during hard weather will hold off some frost at least. When
the straw is finished with in the spring it can be dug into
the ground.

4

The Garden Frame

The beginning of the glazed frame is somewhat obscure but its use certainly followed the mediaeval practice of covering hot-beds with mattresses of straw. Evelyn writing in 1664 describes the use of frames in connection with young trees and during the seventeenth and eighteenth centuries glazed frames were used in the market gardens of this country for the production of early vegetables. In 1781 a writer mentions them as being commonly used and the glass held by means of styles—much as we know them now—for the production of early cauliflowers, salads and other vegetables.

In France the bell glass (cloche) was preferred to the frame by market growers and the latter seems to have been very largely confined to the larger private gardens. Later, however, a small type of frame was brought into use and used with cloches by the French maraicher who eventually brought this type of horticulture to a very high standard. In England the frame was preferred to the cloche.

The development of the greenhouse in this country, however, caused frames to be of rather secondary importance to the market grower, but the English frame of 6 ft. by 4 ft. continued to be popular in most private gardens of any size. In these larger and well equipped gardens very elaborate permanent frames were often seen. Built on a brick base, often as a span-roof structure with greenhouse ventilating gear and pipe heat, they were a feature of the garden and can still be seen in some of the older established gardens.

The English light made of first class timber and of excellent workmanship was an expensive matter when needed in large numbers on the market garden and became less used as more greenhouses were built. In the meantime gardeners in Holland had simplified matters and used what has become known as the Dutch Light. These consisted of one large sheet of glass held in a light rectangular frame. During the summer they were built up into temporary glasshouses for the production of tomatoes.

These Dutch lights were far less costly than the larger and heavier English lights but the standard of joinery was not so good. Nevertheless they were easier to handle and effective in use. They were introduced into this country some sixty years ago and today can be seen in large numbers on most commercial holdings, while the old 6 ft. by 4 ft. light is seldom seen.

A further development in design was brought about after the 1939-45 war when shortage of timber necessitated the use of metal rather than wood in the construction of frames. Many designs and makes can now be had as will be seen in the advertisement pages of any gardening journal. Most are light in weight and can be moved easily if occasion demands.

No garden can be said to be complete in its equipment without a frame and the uses to which it can be put would fill a volume. It is complementary to the greenhouse for there are many greenhouse subjects that, during their early life, are better in the cooler or perhaps shadier conditions of the frame, others that have flowered in the greenhouse are better transferred to the frame for drying off and a resting period. A frame is necessary for hardening off bedding material and for raising and propagating many subjects. Where no greenhouse is available the frame has an added value for much can be done in a good frame that can be done in the greenhouse. Summer bedding plants can be successfully raised; flowering plants can be grown to furnish the dwelling house over the greater part of the year or early vegetables can be produced. The frame can be used during the summer to grow cucumbers or melons and in the autumn and winter stocks of the not quite so hardy subjects can be safely over wintered. A collection of alpines can be ideally housed in a cold frame and be a joy to all who see them in the early spring.

These and other uses for the frame will be found detailed in subsequent chapters.

Before buying or making a frame one should become acquainted with the various types to be had. What are you going to use it for in the main? If it is merely to raise a few seedlings, grow a few lettuce or some early carrots a deep frame will not be necessary. If you have pot plants in mind, French beans or cauliflowers, something with more head room will be necessary. For general purposes a frame 18 in. high at the back and 12 in. at the front will serve, but do not spoil the ship for the sake of a little extra expense. If

• •

The Hartley "10" Glass to ground and built of aluminium alloy. The novel design permits maximum light and solar heat. This type is also available for erection on a 2 ft. 6 in. brick base.

Humex "Circulair" house. entirely new break from the litional design. Adjustable flaps positioned all round base and the adjustable e permits near perfect air-regulation. Constructed aluminium no upkeep is led.

The Oakworth greenhouse Model "D" A really roomy greenhouse the framework being of oak reinforced with tensioned steel rods. Extensions of 3 ft. 7 in. are easily fitted.

The Humex Ventmaster. unit that is entirely automa and will adjust the ventila according to outside weatl conditions and internal tem erature.

Mist Propagation. A thin film of water is automatically sprayed over the cuttings as needed. Soil warming equipment maintains the necessary bottom heat, and cuttings root better and more quickly.

Electric turbo-heaters are simply plugged into a suitable socket. They can be used to warm the house or, in summer, to circulate cool air. The heater should be placed on the floor at a point farthest from the door.

the frame is too deep for a certain purpose the crop can be brought nearer to the top by various means or the frame itself can be raised on another course or two of bricks to accommodate rather taller plants. A temporary framework can always be contrived for a low growing crop.

Frames fall into two main classes : the lean-to and the span-roof types. The most usual is the lean-to type and this may consist of a framework supporting one or more lights. The old type of lean-to will be familiar to all with a 6 ft. by 4 ft. or 4 ft. by 4 ft. light sliding up or down on runners which allow the frame to be opened (Fig. 14).

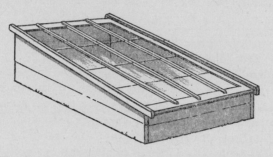

Fig. 14. The English 6 ft. × 4 ft. lean-to frame and light

The span-roof type can be looked on as a mini-greenhouse. At least two lights are needed and these are hinged or fastened in some way at the apex of the roof thus allowing ample room towards the centre for taller growing plants. Light distribution is more even than in the lean-to and ventilation more easily controlled. Such a frame will be more expensive but it will have a greater range of usefulness (Fig. 15).

The walls of a lean-to will vary in height from 1½ to 2½ ft. at the back and from 9 in. to 1½ ft. at the front. The material can be brick, concrete, wood or sometimes asbestos or glass.

The Dutch light has already been mentioned and is now popular both with amateurs and commercial growers. The single sheet of glass is held in a wood frame, the standard size being 59 in. by 30¾ in. overall. The glass slides into rebates in the styles and is secured at the top and bottom by means of short wood cleats. In some cases the top rail is made to the same size as the styles and

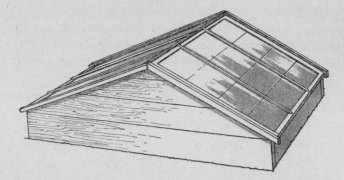

Fig. 15. A span-roof frame will give greater height and a better distribution of light

rebated to take the glass. A cleat is then only needed at the bottom to hold the glass (Fig. 16).

The Dutch light forms a very cheap way of providing light for a frame. When made of cedar no painting or upkeep is necessary except for a coat of linseed oil once a year, and no putty is needed when glazing. The one snag that should be mentioned is the large sheet of glass, but with reasonable care this should not be broken. Heavy P.V.C. is often used instead of glass and can easily be secured to the woodwork.

There are many different designs and makes of metal frames. A feature of many of these is that the glass is brought down to the ground thus admitting all the light that is going. This is all to the

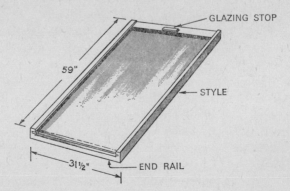

Fig. 16. The Dutch light. One large sheet of glass is held by grooves in the styles. No putty is needed

good for there will be no dark and dank corners, but heat losses are bound to be greater. They can be had in many sizes and both as lean-to or span-roof. They have the merit of mobility and cropping successions can be carried out as with clothes. The metal parts should be sufficiently strong to carry the weight of glass and should be constructed of rustless metal. No upkeep is called for and in most cases the glass simply slides in or is secured with clips.

The Site. For general purposes the frame should be placed in such a position that it gets all the sun that is going. As with cloches warmth from the sun is trapped during the day and absorbed by the soil. If the light is closed down in good time the stored up warmth will be retained and the frame kept warm during the night. Heat losses due to conduction and via any cracks will, of course, occur and for this reason a substantially built frame is to be recommended. A position under a wall or fence facing south or southwest would be ideal. Do not site the frame too near to trees as, apart from the shade they might give, a broken bough or dead wood might fall on the light.

It is essential that the area for frames should be well drained and if necessary it will pay to excavate and place a few inches of hard-core some 18 in. below the surface and refill with a good compost. Where the frame is to be used for standing pots or boxes the area should be level and covered with several inches of sifted ashes and well firmed. A metal frame must be set perfectly level, for any warping of the frame will cause glass breakages. Do not place a frame too near to a fence or wall if this can be avoided but leave room to get behind. If the frame is made of wood it is better to place it on a course of bricks.

Frames are conveniently placed against the greenhouse. Such a site will be protected and it will often be possible to extend the greenhouse heating system for both soil and space warming. A frame is useful on the less sunny side of the house as well as on the sunny side. Here, cooler and more shady conditions can be had when the need arises.

Temporary Frames. A temporary frame can easily be made if a light is available. The height at the back can be 12 to 15 in. and 6 in. at the front. This will allow room for most of the less tall subjects likely to be grown but the actual depth of any frame must depend on the crop to be grown. A slope of approximately 6 in. should be given to the light. The boards, cut to the required length, are nailed or screwed to 2 in. corner pieces.

Dutch lights are handy for making a temporary frame, or indeed a permanent frame and a perfectly good, and certainly the cheapest way is to buy one or two Dutch lights and make a surround to suit your needs. A man handy with tools will have no difficulty in making a concrete frame by means of boards fixed 3 or 4 in. apart to act as a mould and using a four to one mixture of sharp sand and cement. If wood is to be used to make the frame it should be 1 in. in thickness and well painted. Dutch lights can be had from most gardening shops for about 22s. complete with glass.

Continuous cropping can be carried out in the same way as with cloches. A spare range of framing is necessary on which to rest the lights as cropping proceeds and either a single or double span frame can be made to serve.

A double span frame will need less timber—a consideration where a number of lights are being used. A ridge must be arranged for along the centre of the framework and this can be made by driving into the soil lengths of 2 in. by 3 in. timber at 6 ft. intervals. These posts should be cut to a length of 2 ft. 9 in. and driven into the ground leaving the top 18 in. above the soil. A board 1 in. thick and 4 in. wide is nailed along the top of the posts and a 1 in. by 1 in. strip nailed along the centre. Using an unglazed frame as a gauge the front supports on either side can be fixed and then, finally, the ends (Fig. 17).

The lights must be secured in some way and the simplest way is to wire them together over the ridge. The bottom or front ends of the lights can be secured against wind by passing a wire over the wood stop at the bottom of the light and passing it under a hook or screw fixed on the front board. One wire can be used to secure the whole of the lights and be fastened to a stout eye in the side. The posts should be treated with a wood preservative, but not creosote.

Cleanliness and Care. The successful use of the frame will depend a great deal on cleanliness and general hygiene. Too often the frame can become a dumping place for all sorts of gardening rubbish. A few old and dirty pots, seed boxes of old soil, decaying plants, old stakes and a few weeds all go to provide a comfortable home and breeding place for pests and a centre of infection for disease. The keen gardener will find a use for the frame throughout the year but

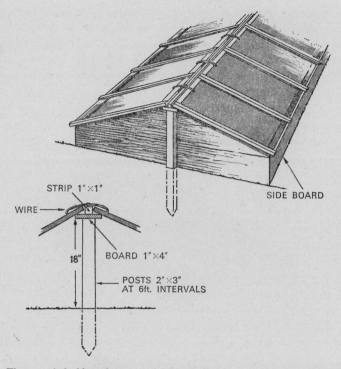

STRIP 1″×1″

WIRE

18″   BOARD 1″×4″

POSTS 2″×3″
AT 6ft. INTERVALS

SIDE BOARD

Fig. 17. A double-span range of Dutch lights showing method of erection

if it must be vacant for a time it should be left clean, preferably with the light off.

As with the greenhouse a frame needs a certain amount of up-keep. The glass must be kept clean, woodwork repainted from time to time and any loose putties renewed and broken glass replaced. Brick or concrete walls will need scrubbing and limewashing. When being repainted the frame should be lifted off the ground by means of blocks or upended so that the bottom edge can be dried and repainted.

Ventilation and Shading. Ventilation is highly important and must never be neglected. Over-watering and too little ventilation will inevitably lead to damping off troubles. Always ventilate by open-ing the frame on the leeward side when cold winds prevail. This will sometimes mean tipping the frame sideways. On occasions when there is a great difference between the temperature of the frame and the outside air and condensation takes place, the light should be eased just enough to allow the glass to become clear again. Normally the frame should be ventilated by raising the light at the back by means of a stepped block (Fig. 18).

After a frost there is often a burst of sun and the temperature in the frame will rise quickly. A chink of air should be given right away to prevent too quick a rise. During hot weather a little light shading by way of an old curtain or thin scrim should be given. This, together with ample ventilation will keep the temperature

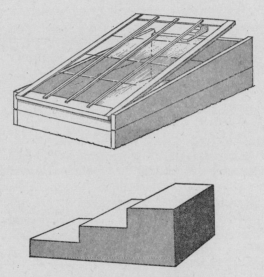

Fig. 18. The normal method of ventilating a frame. A stepped block is handy for propping up the light

within bounds and prevent scorching. Mats will be needed during frosty periods in the winter to maintain warmth.

Heated Frames. The usefulness of the frame can be greatly extended if by some means heat can be applied. The time-old practice of placing the frame on a hot-bed of manure has much to recommend itself but for many the shortage of manure makes this impossible. When fresh manure can be obtained a hot-bed is well worth while, particularly where other methods of heating are not available.

A load of fresh strawy manure is needed and to make up bulk a third of the weight can be added by way of dry leaves. Stack the manure for a week or ten days if it is too fresh, by which time the fiercest of the heat will have gone. The heap should be turned once or twice during the next week and a little water added if necessary. In ten days fermentation should be well on the way and the hot-bed can be made.

The heap should cover an area of about a foot larger all round than the frame to be used, and on this area spread the manure to a depth of about 6 in. mixing in a quantity of leaves. Use one barrowful of leaves to three of manure.

In building the heap use the longest material for the corners and sides and then deal with the middle. Three 6 in. layers of manure and leaves firmed by treading down will be needed to make a good bed. Such a heap will be less fierce than one made entirely of manure but it will last longer. Dry leaves from the previous autumn fall are ideal but leaves long exposed to the weather will be useless.

Once the heap is made the frame should be placed in position and the light left open for a few days to allow any fumes and moisture to escape. Six inches of good soil should now be put into the frame and firmed and left level. Sowing can be done when the temperature falls to 75°F. (24°C.).

Pipe heat can be installed in frames adjoining a heated green-house and both space heating and soil warming (bottom heat) can be had in this way. Three or four 1 in. pipes are fixed round the frames to warm the air and frequently 1 in. pipes laid 12 in. below the surface. The water supply to both space and soil-warming pipes should be separately controlled.

A modern method of heating is by way of electricity. The gardener with little time to spare and where a mains supply is available should seriously consider such a method if he desires to heat his frames. Tubular heaters or special heating cables are fixed round the frame and soil-warming cables are buried some 5 in. below the surface. The installation can be controlled by means of a thermostat and a pre-determined temperature maintained.

The amount of heat needed will depend on the type and size of the frame. If the frame is constructed of brick or concrete or of wood of 1 in. in thickness, a frame 6 ft. by 4 ft. will need two 3 ft. tubular heaters—one at the back and the other at the front. Such an installation, in conjunction with soil warming, will maintain a temperature of 45°F. (7°C.).

For electric soil-warming two types of equipment can be had.

The first is the low voltage system employing a small transformer connected to the mains supply and giving a voltage of from 6 to 12 volts. The warming elements are of bare galvanised wire. The second method is a special mains voltage cable and no transformer is needed. The cost of the first system is more expensive owing to the transformer but as the wires are simply galvanised iron they can be very cheaply replaced, but when a mains cable is damaged replacements will entail a completely new cable.

The cost of running either system is the same. The method recommended is the "dosage" system which simply means that the current is switched on each night and off again the next morning—a matter of eight to ten hours. A loading of 6 watts per square foot is needed—a total of 144 watts for a 6 ft. by 4 ft. frame. This, over the eight or ten hours, would mean just over a unit of electricity per night. Your local Electricity Board will gladly supply full particulars if you are interested. A very helpful booklet can be had entitled "Electricity in the Garden" from the Electrical Development Association, Trafalgar Buildings, 1 Charing Cross, London W.C.1. In any case one should get a competent electrician to carry out the work of bringing the mains supply to the transformer, for although electricity can be a good servant in the garden it can also be a hard master.

There are a number of oil heaters that are suitable for the frame. They will not give a high temperature but they will keep out frost. These are quite satisfactory provided they are kept scrupulously clean and never allowed to smoke. Fumes from a dirty or smoky heater will soon ruin the plants. A chink of air should be left on while the heater is in use.

It will be realised that the use of a frame will entail considerable attention. A day's neglect may ruin a promising batch of seedlings, and neglect to water or shade may easily spell failure and loss of time.

5

Vegetables Under Cloches and Frames

The cultivation of crops under either cloches or frames is much the same and may well be included under one heading. Soil preparation, varieties and sowing and planting technique is again similar except that sowing in the frame must conform to the shape and confines of the frame, whilst sowing under cloches will be done in the normal way by way of rows limited in length only by the number of cloches available. Certain taller growing crops such as peas, broad beans and runner beans to be left to grow *in situ* are obviously more suited to cloche protection.

Warming the soil before sowing as previously mentioned will also apply to frames and during dry weather the soil should be given a good watering before sowing. For the smaller seeds a fine surface tilth is needed. The addition of a half bucketful of moistened peat or sifted compost to each square yard of bed will be an advantage. This will help to retain moisture and improve the texture if it is worked into the top inch or so. See that the soil is reasonably compacted by lightly treading, but the type of soil should be the guiding factor as to how much firming is done. With very early sowings the only firming needed—except on the lightest of soils—will be tamping down after sowing.

When sowing remember that under protection everything is in favour of good germination and the seed should be thinly sown. A light sowing will produce better and sturdier seedlings and less thinning will be necessary. After sowing and covering in lightly tamp along the rows with the back of a rake to ensure that the seeds come into direct contact with the soil. Do not sow too deeply; a shallow drill $\frac{1}{2}$ in. deep is enough for the smaller seeds. When broadcasting the seeds in a frame lightly rake in or give a light covering through a fine sieve and gently firm with a presser.

For cloche or frame work the correct variety is important. For early work choose a variety that will mature quickly, combined with a constitution and habit that makes them responsive to protective measures but hardy enough to put up with the low temperatures they will be subject to at times. Most seedsmen now indicate in some way those varieties suitable for cloche cultivation. Suitable varieties, are discussed in the cultural notes of each subject.

CULTIVATION OF CROPS

Asparagus. An established bed of asparagus can be made to produce very early buds a month or five weeks before the normal time. The bed, or part of the bed, should be cloched in early January after the usual cleaning up and dressing has been done. Cutting should start from the third week in March and the crop can be decloched in late March or early April. Cutting must be discontinued at a correspondingly early date.

If a new bed is being made it can form part of a three or four strip rotation by adopting the method of planting in one straight row and setting the plants 18 in. apart.

Suitable varieties are Early Argenteiul, Connover's Colossal or Kidner's Pedigree for very large buds.

Aubergine. The Egg Plant or aubergine can be grown under cloches but a large cloche raised in some way is needed. The plants should be set out during the first week of June 2 ft. apart on a well prepared site. A low barn will serve for a time but as the plant gains in height a larger cloche will be needed. See also page 158.

Broad Beans. Broad beans can be sown either in early November, late January or early February. The autumn sowing is advisable in the north or exposed districts but in the south an autumn sowing is rather apt to outgrow a low type of cloche during March. Sowings made in the south in late January will soon catch up with those sown in the autumn.

A single row should be sown under tent cloches but two rows can be sown under barns. A wide drill 6 to 8 in. wide and 2½ in. deep should be taken out and the seed sown along either side at staggered intervals of 8 in. In single rows space the seed at 4 in. apart. A further sowing can be made in early March if a succession is needed when one of the Windsor types can be sown and cloched for a short time. A longpod variety is best for early work and can be decloched towards the end of March or early April and grown on in the open in the normal way. A dwarf variety such as Sutton's Dwarf Broad Bean or White Fan can be cloched for a longer period to produce a very early crop. These are much branching varieties and bear large clusters of small pods. Broad beans need a well dressed soil and ample moisture. If the tops are pinched out when the lower clusters of flowers have set the dreaded black fly will be discouraged.

Beans, Dwarf French. The French Dwarf or Kidney Bean is a little hardier than the runner and can be sown earlier. They are however by no means hardy and will need cloche or frame protection until frost danger has passed. They need a warm soil in which to germinate and not too much moisture or the seed will rot, and pre-covering the bed is vitally important.

The first sowing in the south can usually be made during the first week in March and in the north some three or four weeks later. Under cloches a double row should be sown on either side of a 6 in. wide and 2 in. deep drill, staggering the seed along each side at 8 in. intervals. Drop a few extra seeds at one end of the drill to allow for possible replacements. In the frame the seeds should be sown in rows 12 in. apart and the seed placed 6 in. apart.

If the soil is at all acid a dressing of lime should be given, for both beans and peas dislike a soil tending towards sourness. Preparation of the soil should be thorough and organic matter dug in. This can be supplemented with one part dried blood, three parts superphosphate and one part sulphate of potash. This should be worked into the top few inches at the rate of 3 oz. per square yard.

Some growers prefer to sow the seed in boxes in the greenhouse and plant out the seedlings; others chit the seed in damp sand and peat. Whichever method you choose keep the frame closed until germination is had or the seedlings established, when air should be given. During a hot and sunny spell a little light shading will help and once flowering starts water can be given more generously and the foliage sprayed over with clear water occasionally.

The earliest sowings should provide pickings from mid-June and cropping will be had over some weeks if regular picking is done. With a hot-bed the sowing date can be rather earlier.

A late crop is had under cloches by sowing in the open during the July and cloching towards the end of September.

Varieties to sow : The Prince—a very early variety, and Master-piece a rather more robust variety and a tremendous cropper, but slightly later. Phenix Claudia is a stringless variety and well recommended.

Runner Beans. Few crops are more widely grown than runner beans and early supplies are always welcome. Unfortunately they are by no means hardy, and in the normal way cannot be sown until mid-May and rather later in the north.

Double digging the site is advisable and plenty of organic matter should be dug into the bottom spit as well as the top, plus a complete fertiliser as advised for dwarf beans. The first sowing under cloches is made about mid-April—a little earlier in the more favoured districts, but a fortnight later in the north. The cloches must remain in position until towards the end of May or such time as frost is no longer expected.

Two rows can be sown under barn cloches in drills 10 to 12 in. apart and 2½ in. deep, placing the seed 10 to 12 in. apart in opposite positions. This will fit in with the normal method of staking. As soon as the plants are decloched the row should be securely staked. Stakes are sometimes hard to come by and a system or stringing can be used. Where both stakes and time are at a premium the growing point of each shoot can be pinched out and the plants grown on as low bushy plants, taking care to keep the shoots pinched out so that plenty of laterals are formed. This is not an ideal way of growing runners but such a row will usually crop a week earlier than those on stakes even if a few become bent and some are attacked by slugs.

Hammonds Dwarf Scarlet is a useful variety in this connection. It is early and can be grown without stakes, being non-trailing and carrying long straight pods well above the ground.

Plenty of water is needed when the pods begin to swell and at this time frequent syringing with clear water will be appreciated. A mulch between the plants will help to maintain the cool and moist root conditions they like.

Kelvedon Wonder is an excellent variety for cloche work. It is early as also is Princeps but crops over a longer period and bears larger pods If you want pods a yard long for the show bench you must grow one of the maincrop varieties but they will not be so early. Clochcd beans should be ready for picking about mid-July.

Early sowings can be made in deep boxes in the frame. The

plants are set outdoors in the normal way towards the end of May. For both frame and cloches the seed can be chitted in mild heat in a mixture of peat and sand before sowing. The seeds in this case should be carefully sown when the radical appears.

Beetroot. A supply of young fresh beetroot at an early date will be appreciated by those who like them as a separate dish or added to a salad. It is a vegetable that must be grown quickly and without check if it is to be had at its best.

Beetroot is an excellent crop for both frame and cloches and a first sowing can be made at the end of February or early March in the south and at the end of March in the north. One of the early round varieties should be chosen such as Crimson Globe or Selected Detroit Globe. Small successional sowings should be made rather than one large sowing, but protection will not be needed after April. The roots should be drawn and eaten when they are rather larger than golf balls.

A well worked soil is needed that was dressed for a previous crop and no fresh manure must be used but a 3 oz. per square yard dressing of some complete fertiliser should be worked into the top soil. Seed must be sown sparsely as each "seed" is really a capsule containing several seeds. Under barn cloches three rows can be sown with 5 in. between the rows. In the frame the seed can be broadcast or sown in rows. Thin out in good time and leave the seedlings at approximately 4 in. apart.

Cabbage. Young spring cabbage or cabbage greens can be had at a very early date if cloches or frame room is available. The seed is sown at the normal time in July or August and the plants put out in late September or early in October and cloched in early December. Two rows of a small growing variety such as Early Offenham, Ellam's Early Dwarf or Early Market can be grown under barns and if the plants are set at 7 in. apart alternate plants can be cut as spring greens during February or March and the remainder left to mature. The cloches can be taken away in late March. Where a frame is available it can be planted out as suggested and alternate plants cut as greens.

A sowing of cabbage can also be made in the frame or under a cloche or two towards the end of January in the south and the plants put out in the open in March or early April. If a quick maturing variety is used in heads will follow nicely after the first of the spring cabbage. This sowing can be particularly useful when the spring cabbage fails to come safely through the winter. Velocity or Greyhound—a nicely pointed cabbage—are good varieties for this sowing.

Cauliflowers. This is the Queen of all the brassicas and as such demands careful treatment and will take more fussing over than any other vegetable.

The earliest supplies are had from sowings made during September in the frame or under cloches. The seedlings should be pricked out as soon as they can be handled and set 3 in. apart each way. The pricking out bed must be well worked and firmed but do not add any manure. A light dressing of a complete fertiliser with a high potash ratio should be worked into the top few inches of the soil and just before pricking out give a dusting of hydrated lime. Close the frame until the seedlings recover from the move and then give a chink of ventilation and increase this whenever possible but close the light at night and cover with a mat if frost threatens. Also cover any cloches protecting cauliflower seedlings. Any check should be avoided but at the same time the seedlings must be grown on sturdily. Seedlings can also be potted up into 3 in. pots and plunged in ashes up to the rims in a frame.

In March the plants are set out under cloches or in frames. Barn cloches will accommodate two rows 10 in. apart with the plants set at 15 in. in the rows. Under lights, space the plants at 15 in. Ample ventilation should be given once the plants become established. Lights and cloches can come off altogether towards the end of April or early May and good curds should be had by early June.

A sowing is also made in late January to provide heads for summer cutting. Prick out as before and plant out in the open in early April. A brief period of cloche protection will help after planting out.

Cauliflowers must have plenty of manure and ample water supplies. They are gross feeders and thirsty subjects. Always loosen up the plants before taking them from the bed and plant with a trowel—not a dibber.

An early and compact variety is needed. All the Year Round and Improved Snowball are favourites for these sowings.

Capsicum. A vegetable much used on the Continent and fast becom-

ing more popular in this country. Certain varieties are very pun-
gent in flavour and used to make pepper and unless you want them
for pickling or pepper do not grow Cayenne or Chilli but choose
one of the sweet peppers such as Ruby King, Bull Nose Red, etc.
The "peppery" ones, however, are very ornamental.

Capiscum belongs to the same family as the tomato and the
plants are raised and grown very much in the same way. Sow in
the greenhouse in heat in March for planting out in a deep frame
or under large cloches in late May or early June. Prick out the seedlings into 3 in. pots and plant out 18 in. apart in a single row under
cloches or 18 in. apart in the frame. Pick off the first few star-like
flowers in order to encourage the plant to flower more freely, and
as soon as a number of flowers are out give all the ventilation
possible. Ample water supplies will now be needed as the flowers set
and a syringing over with clear water in the evening will help the
plant and discourage red spider.

Cropping should start in early August and the curiously shaped
and wrinkled fruits are picked when large enough and while still
green.

Carrots. Young carrots are a great treat after a long spell of stored
roots and will be one of the first vegetables to be sown under lights
or cloches in the early days.

A light soil is best for the earliest of sowings and a site that was
well dressed for a previous crop should be chosen. Some old compost can be worked into the ground plus a 3 to 4 oz. per square
yard dressing of a complete fertiliser. A dressing of moistened peat
worked into the top few inches will be well worthwhile.

Sowings can be made as early as late January in the south but in
the North early February will be soon enough. Under cloches four
or five rows can be sown under barns. Sow in quite shallow drills
and very sparsely when little thinning out will be needed. In the
frame the seed can be broadcast using approximately ⅛ oz. of seed
per light. It makes for thinner sowing if some sand is mixed with
the seed. Alternatively sowings can be made in drills.

Plenty of ventilation will be necessary once germination is had
but in the early days close the frame at night and give extra cover if
frost is forecast. Weeds can be a nuisance but if a pre-emergence
week-killer is sprayed over the bed a few days before germination is
due the crop can be kept clean for some time. In early April the

cloches or lights can come off and the carrots should be ready during May.

A late sowing towards the end of July in the open and given protection in October will ensure a crop of young carrots during the autumn.

Varieties to sow : Amsterdam Forcing, Ideal or Early Nantes.

Celery—Self-Blanching. Where very early heads of celery are wanted the type known as "self-blanching" should be grown. It is raised in heat in the same way as the standard varieties but it is planted on the flat instead of in trenches and having to be earthed up.

The earliest crops are set out under cloches or frames in mid-April 6 in. apart. Three rows can be planted under barn cloches. When the leaves reach the roof glass—which will be towards the end of May—the cloches can come off but in the more exposed districts it may be necessary to give a larger cloche for a short time. The lights of the frame can be removed at the end of May or the frame raised on a few bricks to give another few inches of head-room. The plants are self-blanching and no tying is needed but much depends on the plants being grown closely together.

The soil for this crop cannot be too rich and unless plenty of organic matter is present and the soil highly fertile the crop will be a poor one. It is also a crop that must have ample water supplies. In rich and moist conditions good and well flavoured heads will be had from early August onwards.

Blanching is helped by working straw in between the plants and round the outside. The straw can be held in place by means of low wire netting. A deep frame is ideal for this crop.

The variety to grow is Golden Self-Blanching.

Courgettes. See Vegetable Marrow.

Cucumbers. Both cloches and frames are suitable for growing cucumbers during the summer months. The earliest plants must be raised in heat in early April and planted out at the end of May or in early June.

Cucumbers need a rich bed and for economy in manure separate stations can be made. For cloches they should be 3 ft. apart. Take out two or three spades full of soil and replace with strawy manure or good compost. Firm and finish off with a low mound of fertile soil to which some complete fertiliser has been added.

The best method of training under cloches is to pinch out the growing point just beyond the fourth or fifth leaf to encourage early laterals to form. Select the two best laterals and stop them at the fifth or sixth leaf and cut out any unwanted shoots. The two laterals should be trained in each direction of the cloches. Sub-laterals will soon appear and bear the majority of the fruits. Fruit bearing shoots should be stopped at two leaves beyond the fruit. Any non-fruiting shoots should be stopped at the fourth leaf, and male flowers should be picked off. Feeding will be necessary after the first flush, and then at fortnightly intervals, with a high nitrogen fertiliser.

Where a heated frame or a hotbed is available a rather earlier start can be made and with a hotbed it will be sufficient to make a mound of good soil on top. Otherwise prepare the frame as for cloches. The average size of frame will accommodate one plant, usually placed in the centre.

Training in the frame is done by stopping at the fourth or fifth leaf and the resulting laterals trained towards each corner and stopped when they near the frame. Further training will be similar to that of cloched cucumbers.

It is essential to maintain a humid atmosphere and that the bed should be kept moist but never sodden. Syringe the plants and surrounds with aired water twice a day giving the second syringing late in the afternoon and closing up the frame, but some discretion will be needed on dull or wet days. Little ventilation will be needed except during hot and sunny weather but normally the light should be raised an inch or two at the back. Shading will be necessary.

Several of the house type of cucumbers can be grown in the frame or under cloches. Telegraph, Butcher's Disease-Resisting or Conqueror are suitable. Ridge cucumbers are sometimes preferred and can be planted out under protection at the end of April, but the earlier plants must be raised in heat. For later cutting seed of a ridge type can be sown *in situ* under lights or cloches in late April. Perfection or Hampshire Giant are good varieties (see also page 143).

Endive. Endive makes a welcome change from lettuce and is particularly valuable in the late autumn. There are two main types—Curled and Batavian. The latter is hardier than Curled and more suitable for cloche work. It looks very much like a cos lettuce and is grown in the same way.

For winter production sowings should be made during July and August in the open. Two rows can be grown under barn cloches, the plants being spaced at 10 in. apart in the rows. There will be no need to cloche the plants until the end of September. Curled varieties are better grown in the frame.

Endive must be blanched or the flavour will be bitter. First tie loosely as with cos lettuce and thickly coat the glass with a dark distemper on the underside or cover with a large flowerpot—not forgetting to cover up the drainage hole. The heads must be dry when cloching, tying up, or covering is done. Only cloche a few at one time, as when blanching is complete the heads soon deteriorate. Blanching will take from three to four weeks.

When nearing maturity the heads can be lifted and replanted in the frame for blanching. Cover the light with sacks or black polythene but ventilate whenever frost is not anticipated.

Ruffec or Moss Curled are good varieties of the curled type and have very finely divided leaves. Green Batavian or Carter's Oval-leaved are excellent varieties of the Batavian type.

Garlic. So often garlic cannot be planted in the open soon enough to ensure full growth and proper harvesting. Under cloches planting can be done in the less exposed areas in late January or early February. Cloches will only be needed for a few weeks but they should be replaced for another short period towards the end of July to ensure good harvesting.

When planting divide the bulb into its separate segments or "cloves". Each bulb will have some ten to twelve cloves and each of these, except the centre ones, will produce a bulb. Plant them 6 in. apart under a few cloches as you would shallots. Soil and cultivation will be the same as for shallots or onions.

Lettuce. Cloches and frames are ideal for lettuce production and it is possible to cut well hearted heads some four to six weeks earlier than from normal sowing outdoors. In the autumn the season can be extended into November or even December in the milder districts.

The most important sowing both for the frame and under cloches is in mid-October. A date between the second and the fourth week is the best time, but in the north the last week in September would be better. In mild districts the end of October is not too late.

It is important to select the right variety of lettuce. Lettuces are long day plants and need long hours of daylight. Certain varieties have been bred to respond to shorter hours of light and one of these must be chosen. May King or May Queen—they are both the same—is a suitable variety and was once the most popular, but on account of a slight tinge that often shows on the outer leaves it is sometimes objected to although the flavour or texture is not affected. Newer varieties without any trace of a reddish tinge can be had. Attractie, Knap, Delta, Winterpride and Cloek are all suitable for this sowing. French Frame does very well in the more southern districts.

Sowing can be made *in situ* and thinned out or the seed sown in a seed-bed and the seedlings planted out during December. The sowing is made under cloches or frames. When sown *in situ* early thinning out is necessary but the final thinning may be left until early February. Two rows are sown under cloches of the barn type. In the frame plant 9 to 10 in. apart.

When planting out handle the seedlings very carefully to avoid bruising and see that the tap root goes straight down. Avoid planting too deeply—the seed leaves should just clear the ground, but only just. The crop will need coverage until late March or early April in the south and rather later in the north. From this sowing large heads will be ready in late March or early April.

Those who prefer cos lettuce will find Lobjoits Green or Winter Density suitable varieties for sowing either in the autumn or in early February. They are both self-folding and need no tying but will mature a little later than the cabbage type. Where both cabbage and cos varieties are needed a row of cos can be sown or planted between the cabbage varieties.

Another sowing is made in late January or early February in the south. These will follow very closely after the autumn sown crop. Feltham King, Borough Wonder or Unrivalled are suitable for this sowing. Late February will be a more suitable date in the north.

Sowings made in March can be given protection for a short time with advantage especially in the north but generally speaking protection is unnecessary after mid-April.

As far as protection is concerned the next sowing is made in mid-August in the open for coverage in late September. Unrivalled or Winterpride can be sown. A sowing can be made with a view to cloching or in such a way that it will conform to the size of a light frame and the frame moved over in September. This sowing will provide cutting during the autumn, and in mild districts well into November and even December.

Lettuce must have a good fertile soil but for October sowing a site manured for a previous crop is best as the aim must be to grow the plants on as sturdily as possible. A light side dressing of sulphate of ammonia or nitrate of soda given in February will act as a fillip. Ventilation must be given whenever weather permits but have mats or hessian ready to cover the glass in case of hard frost.

Mint. For early supplies dig up some of the old roots in November or December and after washing off the soil cut them up into small pieces and plant 1 in. deep in a prepared strip as wide as the cloches. One cloche with the ends closed will probably be all that is needed. Young mint will be had in the very early spring. Roots can also be planted in a deep box and stood in the frame.

Mustard and Cress. See page 160.

Onions. Where bulb onions are concerned cloches are extremely useful as they permit very early sowing in the spring and towards the end of the season the cloches can be replaced for a while to ensure thorough ripening and good harvesting. Sowings made in the late summer for overwintering can be cloched during October and onward to secure a safe passage through the winter.

The earliest sowings can be made in late January or early February under cloches or in deep boxes in the frame for transplanting in late March and a sowing can also be made *in situ* under cloches.

An early or late supply of salad onions can be had under cloches or frames from sowings made in late January or February and again in mid-August. The late crop should be cloched during October for pulling during the late autumn and winter. White Lisbon is the best variety of salad onion.

Parsnip. Gardeners in the north will find it an advantage to cloche a few rows of parsnips. Earlier sowings will be possible and the cloches can be removed when the seedlings are well up and established. During inclement weather in the south and especially on the heavier soils a brief period of cloche protection will ensure early sowings.

Parsley. The spring sowing of parsley will be less difficult to get going if a sowing is made under a cloche or two. The greatest benefit in clocling this herb is had by covering during October a few plants from a sowing made at the end of July. In this way fresh parsley will be available throughout the winter.

Peas. Peas are a general favourite and an early dish is always welcome. The first sowing is made in October in the north and November in the south. This sowing must be cloched throughout the winter and one of the dwarf round-seeded varieties chosen. Meteor, Feltham First and Eight weeks are all very dwarf and can be grown under a high type of cloche until ready to pick in early may.

Except in the more exposed districts another sowing can be made in late January or February. The same varieties can again be sown but if the crop is to be decloched in early April a less dwarf variety may be sown. Kelvedon Wonder, Early Onward or Laxton's Superb are good varieties. A successful sowing made in March can be cloched to help quick germination and will only need the cloches until the seedlings are well advanced.

A late sowing is made in mid-July in the open and given cloche protection in late September or early October. Meteor will again be the best variety for this late sowing and a high type of cloche will be necessary. This late crop will need plenty of ventilation and the base of the plants must be kept free from annual weeds which can form a constantly damp carpet round the plants. Mildew must be watched for and the plants should be dusted with Kara-thane or sulphur to ward off any attack. The seed should be sown rather less thickly than for a spring sowing.

A good crop of peas can be grown on most soils provided it is deeply worked and plenty of manure or other organic matter dug in. Sowing is done in wide drills $2\frac{1}{2}$ in. deep and the seed scattered over the width of the drill at intervals of 2 to 3 in.

When the seedlings are some 3 in. high small twiggy sticks should be placed alongside to support the plants and the haulm staked in the normal way as soon as the plants are decloched. Ample water supplies will be needed especially when the pods begin to swell.

Early peas are often raised in the frame in deep boxes or pots for planting out later. The seed can also be inserted into strips of turf and in due course planted out.

Radish. Only small successional sowings should be made and the best way is to treat the crop as a catch or inter-crop. Seed can be sown alongside many crops or between carrots, turnips, beet, etc. Sow thinly in drills ½ in. deep. The radishes will be ready to pull in a very short time and will not interfere with the main crop. Sowings in late January or February will provide material for the salad bowl when radishes are expensive to buy. If they are grown on their own a low barn will cover five or six rows or the seed can be broadcast over the area and lightly raked in.

Sowings made in late September, October and November will provide good radishes if given frame or cloche protection. When sowing carrots, turnips, etc. in the frame or under cloches mix in a few radish seeds. They will act as markers for the rows as they quickly germinate and when sizable can be pulled and eaten.

Scarlet Globe, French Breakfast and Saxa are good varieties and add colour to a salad.

Spinach. Two types of spinach can be had : the round or summer spinach and prickly or winter spinach. Prickly spinach is hardier, much less inclined to run to seed and just as tender as the round type when well grown. It should always be used for cloche cultivation.

A fertile soil, rich in humus is needed and during dry weather plenty of water should be given. Prickly spinach can be grown in most districts during the winter without protection but the leaves are very liable to become coarse and dirty and in cold weather growth will be slow. Under cloches continuous pickings can be had through the winter from successional sowings made in September and October and often in November and January.

Two rows can be sown under barn cloches in drills 1 in. deep. Thin the seedlings to stand at 6 in. apart. Generous sowings should be made if any quantity is needed for a liberal picking is needed for a dish. If only a few plants are available one is inclined to defoliate the entire plant, but if only two or three leaves are taken the plant is not unduly weakened and will continue to produce fresh leaves.

Sweet Corn. Sweet or Sugar Corn is easy enough to grow but it is not so easy to get first class cobs at a reasonably early date in our uncertain climate and cultivation becomes somewhat of a gamble. Fortunately hybrid varieties can be had that are more suited to our climate and with these and early protected sowings it is possible to enjoy cobs by mid-July.

Sweet corn is only half-hardy and cannot be sown outdoors until frost danger has passed. Plants are sometimes raised in the greenhouse but sweet corn resents in no uncertain terms transplanting and often fails. Under lights or cloches the seed can be sown *in situ* during the second or third week in April. Sow on well prepared ground—preferably ground manured for a previous crop—giving a dressing of 3 to 4 oz. per square yard of a high grade fish manure or some other complete fertiliser. Choose a sunny spot for although it is a short day plant and does most of its growing at night it likes its daylight hours to be sunny and warm.

Two rows are sown under barn cloches along 1½ in. deep drills 12 in. apart and the seed dropped at staggered intervals of 12 to 15 in. along the rows. This is wide enough planting for the John Innes Hybrid but later and more robust varieties need 15 to 18 in. To assist pollination sow several short rows rather than one long single row. Further sowings can be made in the south in May for succession.

Once the seed germinates growth will be rapid and the plants must be decloched or the cloches raised in some way if only for a day or two. Tillers that spring from the base should be left. Pull a little soil up round the base of the plants to encourage buttress roots to form and if the site is at all exposed it is as well to give a little support against strong winds by driving in a stake here and there along the rows and tying strong fillis from stake to stake.

Each plant will produce two good cobs which should be ready from about the third week in July from the earliest sowings. In more northern districts where sowings must wait until a later date the time of maturity will, of course, be later. Further north it will indeed be a gamble as to whether the crop succeeds.

Sweet corn must be eaten while it is still fresh. A cob left for thirty-six hours may have 60 per cent of its sugar content converted to starch. It is not easy to judge just the right time to cut. Look for the withering silks hanging from the tip of the cobs. When these are a dark brown and well withered, open the sheath of a likely cob and squeeze one of the seeds with the thumb nails.

A watery exudate will indicate that the cob is not ready but if milky the cob should be just right. A thick creamy fluid means that cutting is already overdue. When a cob is found to be just right the condition of the silks should be noted and other cobs cut when the silks present the same degree of withered browness.

A frame can be used to start off a block of sweet corn. Sow as recommended for cloches. If the frame is of a portable nature it can be lifted off towards the end of May and used elsewhere for cucumbers or melons.

One of the earliest varieties and probably the only one really suited to the more northern districts is the John Innes Hybrid. North Star and Prima are also hybrids and suitable for early work. Golden Bantam—largely used for canning—is a little later in maturing but an excellent variety.

Tomato. The outdoor tomato crop depends so much on the weather that it can become very much a gamble, especially as planting cannot be undertaken until frost danger has passed. With cloches or a frame a start can be made during the second week in April and thus give a much longer period of growth.

Under cloches there are two main methods used. Plants can be set out under cloches until late May or early June when they can be decloched and staked in the ordinary way and grown on as outdoor plants. During September the stakes are taken away and the plants laid down on straw and cloched again to hasten the ripening of any green fruits that are left.

The second method is to keep the plants cloched throughout the summer. A high cloche is needed but if the plants are set in a 6 in. trench it will allow just that much extra height. Adaptors on which to place the cloches can be had that will give an additional 12 in. of height. The first method does quite well in the southern half of the country but in the north the second method will be the best although it does mean more trouble.

The plants for an April planting will have to be propagated in a warm greenhouse or ordered from a reliable nurseryman. If only a few plants are needed it is better to buy them. Sturdy, short-jointed plants are needed, for a good start is everything. Only one row can be grown under the cloches and before planting be sure that the plants have not come straight from a warm house but have been given cool treatment for a time. Set the plants 18 in. apart and give a short cane to each for temporary support. By the end of May when the cloches are removed the first truss will be well advanced and a permanent stake should be given right away.

The second method calls for a little extra training. In order to keep the plants low they can be grown on two stems. Two short stakes or canes are needed : an upright one and an oblique one. The main stem is trained up the diagonal stake and stopped one leaf beyond the third truss and an early lateral taken up the vertical stake and stopped one leaf beyond the second truss (Fig. 19).

Bush varieties can be cloched throughout their growth with little trouble with a smaller type of cloche if a variety such as Puck is chosen. Amateur is another good bush but makes rather a

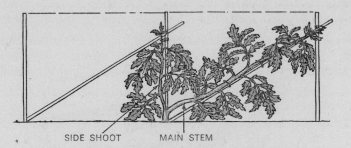

SIDE SHOOT   MAIN STEM

Fig. 19. A method of training tomatoes under large cloches

larger plant. Plant in the normal way but give a good mulch of straw as the lower trusses may touch the ground.

Where on account of unsuitable soil conditions it has been impossible to grow tomatoes in the garden the ring cultured method can be used and combined with the second method described (see page 141).

There are several ways in which the frame can be used for tomatoes. Plants can be raised in the frame but they will not be so early as those from a warm house unless a heated frame with soil warming can be used. Plants can also be planted in the frame and trained horizontally on canes from front to back. The frame must be reasonably deep and most permanent frames will accommodate three plants. Lastly when the frame has been cleared of early crops it can be upended and stood against a wall or fence to protect three tomato plants in pots or boxes. The light is stood in front and secured with a stout wire so arranged that ventilation is permitted at the top or to allow the light to be taken away (Fig. 20).

Most standard varieties will respond to cloche or frame cultivation. Where a variety is known to succeed in any one district it is worth trying under cloches. Early varieties are obviously needed and those best suited for outdoor cultivation. Harbinger and Hundredfold are good varieties and Moneymaker—an old and tried variety free from greenback. Of the newer varieties Eurocross has done very well under cloches. Clucas 99 is popular in the north as is also Woodwood's Open Air which is very short jointed.

Alicantie is a newer variety that succeeds well in the open as well as in the greenhouse.

Turnip. It is no good sowing turnips too early for they must be grown quickly and without check at any stage or they will become

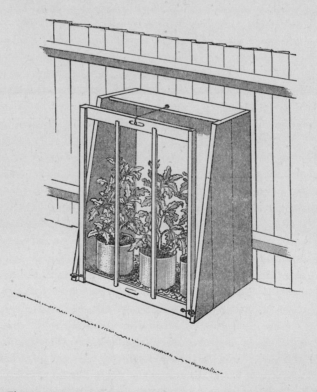

Fig. 20. Two or three tomato plants can be protected by means of an up-ended frame. The light should be secured top and bottom but removed as necessary

woody. Cloches or frames permit a sowing to be made in late February or early March if the weather is favourable. In the north the end of March or early April will be safer. Sow in rows 5 in. apart. Three rows can be sown under barn cloches. Give an initial thinning in good time and eventually leave to stand at 4 in. apart. Keep the soil moist during growth and use the roots when they are little bigger than golf balls. Decloching can be done towards the end of April in the south.

The same procedure can be followed in the frame but a start can be made a little earlier if the frame is heated. In the frame the seed is often broadcast but some skill is needed in making a sparse and even sowing. Keep the soil moist and give air whenever possible. The light can come right off towards the end of April.

Vegetable Marrow. Preparation of the soil should be similar to that needed for cucumbers and melons and separate stations should be prepared 3 ft. apart. A start can be made in mid-April with plants previously raised in a warm greenhouse. Seeds can be sown *in situ* under cloches or frames at the end of April. Bush varieties are to be preferred and either White or Green Bush can be grown as they need less room than the trailing kinds. Two plants can be planted in the average size of frame.

Cloches and lights must be left in position until frosts are no longer feared and with the earlier plantings hand pollination may be necessary. Give plenty of water and a liquid feed once a week when the marrows begin to swell. Small marrows of 12 in. in length are best and should be had from the middle of June.

Courgettes are becoming increasingly popular and are grown in exactly the same way as vegetable marrows. A true courgette should be grown such as Courgette or Zucchini. An immense crop of small marrow-like fruits is produced and should be cut when 4 in. in length and cooked whole. The secret in getting a continuity of tiny fruits is to keep cutting and never leave them to grow large. The spacing need not be quite so generous as for marrows.

Strawberries. It is convenient to mention strawberries in connection with frames and cloches under this heading for they are without doubt one of the favourite crops for forwarding especially under cloches. Forcing is another matter and will be found under greenhouse work on page 171.

Cloche and frame cultivation calls for a rather different technique to that needed for open beds and the plants are treated as annuals. This permits more plants to be grown on a given area and advantage can be taken of the fact that the earliest and finest fruits are had when treated as annuals; but it does mean that rooted runners must be planted earlier than would be the normal practice and the plants are not de-blossomed but allowed to produce their fruits during the next spring.

Rooted runners should be ordered and planted out on a prepared bed during August so that they can become well established before the hard weather sets in. A barn cloche will cover two rows 10 in. apart and the plants are set at staggered intervals of 12 in. See that the soil is well moistened before planting.

There is no need to cover the plants until early February in the north and mid-February in the south—for they are very hardy indeed. The cloches will warm up the soil and stimulate root action but before cloching clean up the bed and refirm any plants that have been lifted by frost. At the same time hoe in a 2 oz. per yard run of sulphate of potash.

The plants will soon respond to the protective covering and start to flower. Pollination will not suffer for small insects rather than bees will do this, but somehow whenever bees are about they will be seen under the glass however tightly the cloches seem to be butted together.

It is better to leave the cloches or lights on until fruiting is over but ventilation and some shading should be given as the weather becomes warmer. Too high a temperature will quickly spoil the fruit. The cloches can be spaced to give extra ventilation but not so widely that birds will easily get in or more fruit may be spoiled than you will gather. For the same reason do not remove the end pieces. Picking should commence in early May.

An early variety that is not too leafy is needed and of course, of good flavour. Cambridge Favourite is now more widely grown than any under cloches but newer varieties such as Vigour and Redgauntlet can be well recommended. The last named is a little later in cropping. A good strain of Royal Sovereign can be grown. This is more leafy than those mentioned and a little later but of delicious flavour.

Remontant varieties are planted in October 18 in. apart. These should be de-blossomed in the spring and will then go on fruiting from late July until well into November or, in mild districts, into December if given cloche coverage in late September or early October. Sans Rivale or Triomphe are good varieties of these late fruiting kinds.

Nearly all strawberries are very prone to virus diseases and for this reason only plants from certified stocks should be planted. It is unwise to accept runners from a friend unless the stock is known to be clean and healthy.

Melons. Here is a useful crop, and not nearly so difficult to grow as is often thought. It is one that will occupy the frame throughout the summer and can be grown quite well under cloches. Unfortunately it is not a crop for the more northern grower.

Good soil preparation is essential for melons are gross feeders and stations as recommended for cucumbers should be prepared. An old hot-bed in the frame will be ideal. The plants will need to be raised in heat in a greenhouse or heated frame and the seed sown some five weeks before planting out is due. Plant out at the end of May or early June having first well moistened the soil. Under cloches plant at 3 ft. intervals or in the centre of the frame.

The initial training is much the same as for cucumbers. Stop the plant at the fourth or fifth leaf and the resulting laterals at 15 to 18 in. Under cloches train the two best in either direction along the cloche row and cut out the unwanted laterals. In the frame train a lateral towards each corner. In either case the laterals must be stopped to encourage sub-laterals which will bear the fruit.

The tiny yellow flowers will soon appear, some with a little melon behind the petals. These are the female flowers and must be pollinated. Hand pollination should be carried out with the earlier crops and a number of flowers should be dealt with at one time. Later on insects will do this quite well with the varieties suggested. Once the embryo melons start to swell reduce the number to two or three and stop the shoot two leaves beyond the melon. Stop non-fruiting shoots at two or three leaves and pinch out any further fruits that appear. Ripe melons should be ready towards the end of August.

Throughout growth and particularly when the fruits are swelling a moist root run and a humid atmosphere is needed. The varieties recommended will not be so fussy about this as some of the house melons but regular syringing over with aired water during normal summer weather will be needed and the glass will need a light shading. Further details as to this and final ripening will be found under greenhouse culture on page 166 and 167.

For frames or cloches Dutch Net, Tiger and Copenhagen Market can be recommended.

6

Flowers Under Cloches and Frames

The flower enthusiast should never think that low coverage must be confined to vegetables and fruit. Indeed, a high proportion of the early flowers seen in the shops are grown under lights or cloches and there is still much room for experiment in this direction.

One of the chief advantages of low coverage is that the protection afforded permits sowing or planting at an earlier date or over-wintering under more favourable conditions and correspondingly earlier blooming. Where supplies of flowers for indoor decorations are needed a very small part of the vegetable garden can be set aside to serve for what our American friends call a "cutting" garden. Here various plants can be grown under a frame or two or a row of cloches. Economy in space is had as the plants can be grown in rows closely together without any attempt at display or arrangement as would be usual in the border. Nor will a carefully designed border be robbed of its beauty.

In this way hardy annuals can be safely overwintered with a view to early flowering; winter flowering subjects such as anemones and violets can be grown and many kinds of bulbs and corms will provide a wealth of bloom well ahead of normal outdoor plantings. Early flowering chrysanthemums and dahlias can be given a longer period of flowering by reason of earlier planting.

The following list by no means exhausts the possibilities of flowers under low coverage but it should be a guide to the more popular plants that will be helped in one way or another by using protective measures.

Anemones. As frame or cloche users we are mostly concerned with the winter production of these fascinating and popular flowers. It is only in the mildest districts of the south coast and south-west that anemones can be flowered successfully in the open during the winter months. Elsewhere in the more southern districts protection will be needed.

The two chief kinds grown for winter production are the St. Brigid which bears semi-double flowers in a wide range of pastel shades and the somewhat hardier De Caen—a single flower in a variety of strong colours. This is the anemone grown so largely for the cut flower trade. They are grown from seed or corms but it is far better and more convenient to grow them from small corms or "pips" of from 2 to 3 or 3 to 4 cms. These small corms produce a more vigorous plant than the larger corms and flower over a longer period.

The corms are sown early in July for it is essential to have a well developed plant before the harder weather sets in. Two row 10 in. apart are grown under barn cloches or planted in rows in the frame. Sow in drills 1½ in. deep and place three corms in the form of a small triangle at intervals of 12 in. They are also sown 4 in. apart but the former method will facilitate weeding. Sow in the open and give coverage early in october if weather dictates. The important thing is to get the plants protected before any severe weather can do any damage.

Anemones belong to the buttercup family (Ranunculaceae) and succeed best in a good loam but any fertile soil will grow good plants so long as it is well drained and well supplied with organic matter. A dressing of 4 oz. per square yard of fish manure should be worked into the top few inches of soil before the corms are sown.

Anemones are reasonably hardy and resent close conditions. They must have ample ventilation whenever possible but they will not be happy in strong winds. On no account must the soil be allowed to dry out during early growth and the bed must be kept free from weed growth. They are very shallow rooters and only light hoeing must be done. Larger weeds near the plants are better cut out carefully with a knife. Any precocious buds should be picked off, but early in October cutting should start in earnest. Always cut the stems as low down as possible with a sharp knife to avoid disturbing the plants. The flowers should be cut when the colour is well showing but before the bud is fully open.

Annuals. There are a number of hardy annuals that can be sown in the autumn for overwintering and early cutting and here cloches will be found to be the most convenient method of protection as they can be used wherever in the garden it is most convenient to

Gloxinia (Suttons' Perfection) One of the loveliest of greenhouse plants and not at all difficult to grow if warmth and moisture is provided.

A Dutch Light type of house on a concrete base. Constructed of Red Deal or Western Red Cedar. The photograph shows a 20 ft. x 10 ft. house but smaller sizes can be had.

A well designed span-roof house eminently suited to the keen amateur. This is the 'Crewe Mk. 2' supplied by Messrs. R. Hall and Co.

make the sowing. Amongst these hardy annuals are larkspur, nig-ella, cornflowers, calendula and the annual gypsophila. The latter is a most useful subject to mix in with other flowers and can be had well ahead of the perennial gypsophila. In the milder districts clarkia, godetia, sweet sultan and annual scabious can be over-wintered for early cutting. Sowings can also be made in the early spring and given cloche protection for a few weeks.

Seed is sown in mid-September and barn cloches will accom-modate two rows 10 in. apart. Most of the seeds are very small and a fine surface tilth is needed. The site should be one that has been manured for a previous crop, for any sappy growth should be avoided. At this time of the year it may be necessary to well water the site some hours ahead of sowing. Single out the seedlings as soon as they can be handled to avoid overcrowding but leave the final thinning until late February or March. The cloches will not be needed until October or before any hard frost is likely. De-cloching can be done in late March or early April.

With cloche protection both cornflowers and larkspurs will make quite a hedge and some support will be needed in the spring if long straight stems are to be had. This can be done by using pea boughs or by pushing in a stake here and there along the rows and passing thick fillis from stake to stake.

Calendula. Special mention should be made of this useful and early flower. Where very early cutting is needed a sowing made in mid-August will prove very much earlier than one made in September if given frame or cloche protection from October onwards. It can be one of the very first of the spring flowers and most valuable for cutting and bringing indoors. The old Orange King and Radio are still good varieties and bear their flowers on long stems. Thin out to stand at 8 in. apart. With protection an August sowing should pro-vide flowers in February and in a mild season even January.

Chrysanthemum maximum. This perennial is very popular in the early days but it is not at all tolerant of wet conditions and can be cloched from November until April with advantage. This will help to maintain drier conditions and also advance the first flush of blooms. The plants can be divided and replanted during August or early spring. Esther Read, Wirral Supreme and Wirral Pride are good varieties. These are all white. Cobham gold is a light yellow.

Chrysanthemum, Early Flowering. Apart from hardening off prep-
aratory to planting out the chief use of protective covering lies in
making it possible to get the young plants set out in their permanent
quarters at an early date so that early flowering can be assured and
the best of the blooms enjoyed before autumn frosts cut the plants
down. Under cloches the plants can be set out in mid-April instead
of the normal mid-May planting. The first stop can be made as
soon as the plants are established and growing away.

A short period of cloche protection should appeal to gardeners
in the more exposed and colder districts. A little extra height can be
had by planting in a shallow trench or raising the cloches on a few
bricks should this become necessary. Decloche when frost is no
longer a menace. Dutch lights, supported on a framework are used
to protect the blooms in the autumn.

Dahlias. A tender subject that must often wait for favourable
weather before planting out can be done. Old tubers can be planted
out in mid-April and rooted cuttings towards the end of that
month if given cloche protection. This will make for a longer period
of flowering.

Gladioli. Many commercial growers look for the earliest gladioli
from corms planted under lights during February in the south and
early March in the north. Under lights the corms are often planted
between rows of spring lettuce. The rows can be 9 in. apart and the
corms planted 3 in. apart. Where the rows run from back to front
in Dutch light frames eighteen corms can be planted per row. Plant
4 in. deep and line the drill or planting hole with a little sharp
sand. It is usual to plant 12 cm. size corms.

It is usually necessary to have to raise the frame on blocks as
the leaves lengthen and reach the glass but do not leave the light off
altogether until mid-May as the young leaves are tender. The fact
that the base of the plants is exposed will not matter but a curtain
of hessian draped round the frame will tend to hasten flowering.

Cloches are also largely used to start off this crip but unless large
cloches are available it is better not to plant too early. Four rows
can easily be grown under barn cloches and the corns spaced at
4 in. in the rows. Cloches must be removed or raised when the
leaves touch the glass.

Early varieties should be chosen : Allard Pierson (pink), Red Fox (vermillion), Sweet Seventeen (peach) and New Europe (orange scarlet) are well known varieties.

Helleborus. These are hardy plants and the Christmas Rose (*H. niger*) will normally flower round about Christmas but the large white blooms and foliage are so often completely spoiled by mud splashes and by being buffeted about by the wind. A large type of barn cloche placed over an established clump in late November will ensure clean blooms by Christmas.

Helleborus orientalis bears flowers of varying shades of purple, pink and grey. They are also known as Lenten Lilies. Cloching will advance the date of flowering and ensure first class foliage and flowers.

Iris, Dutch. The earliest flowers are had from a planting made in the greenhouse but early supplies can be had from both frames and cloches. Planting is done in late September or October and often as an intercrop between lettuce. Corms of 7 or 8 cm. are best and should be planted 2 in. deep in rows 9 in. apart. The corms are spaced at approximately 2 in. apart. Under barn cloches four rows can be planted, the corms being spaced at 3 in. apart.

There is no need to put the lights on the frame or use the cloches until early December or when the leaves first show. Plenty of ventilation should be given except during frosty weather. Extra height will be needed as the flower stems lengthen if the blooms are to be protected from excessive rain or a late frost.

The variety "Wedgewood" is the earliest and is a light blue. This is followed by Imperator—a darker blue and more suited to cloche coverage than the former. There is also a yellow and a white variety, but the blues are more popular.

The lovely little Iris reticulata can be cloched in January and Iris stylosa (*I. unguicularis*) in November for early flowering.

Lily of the Valley. These lovely and fragrant flowers are well worth having at an early date. An established bed can be covered by a portable frame or a few cloches in early January. Flowers will be had towards the end of April.

If the crop is to be protected it is worth growing well. So often an old bed becomes so hopelessly overcrowded that cropping deteriorates. A fresh start can be made on a new bed in September when the site should be deeply dug and the soil well enriched with leaf mould and well rotted manure or compost. The site should be in partial shade. Single crowns or "pips" are planted 2 in. square the tips being left 1 in. below the surface. The plump round pips are the flowering pips and the ones to select. A mulch of sifted leaf mould and rotted manure should be given each October when cleaning up the bed. Remove the frame or cloches as soon as flowering is over when ample water supplies may be needed.

Fortin's Giant is a fine variety to grow and bears large flowers on long stems.

Narcissi. Where daffodils are needed for cutting a number of bulbs should be given protection to supply early needs. From a special planting a very large number of blooms will be had from quite a small area. Under cloches or lights cutting can be had some three weeks before normal plantings will be ready and at a time when such flowers are expensive to buy. The bulbs are not cheap but a bed will last for three years and when finally lifted a considerable number will be available for replanting and any small bulblets can be grown on in a nursery bed to become flowering bulbs.

Double dig and well dress the site with organic matter but not fresh manure. Into the top few inches work in a 3 oz. per square yard dressing of bone meal and a light dressing of sulphate of potash, or if more convenient give a 4 oz. per square yard dressing of fish manure. A well worked piece of ground manured and limed for a previous crop would be excellent.

Plant in good time. Get the bulbs in during September and plant with a trowel or a bulb planter 3 in. apart in rows 6 in. apart. Under barn cloches plant four rows 5 in. apart and at four inch intervals in the rows. Do not cloche or put the lights on until growth begins to appear. This will be towards the end of January or early February when growth will be rapid. In the north coverage should be given during December. As the flower stems lengthen it will be necessary to raise the frame or the cloches if the flowers are to be grown to maturity.

The flowers need not develop fully under the glass but can be picked at a young stage and finished off indoors. The stage to cut is when the sheath has broken and just exposed the perianth.

Early varieties are needed and the following are very suitable. Golden Harvest, Magnificence, Fortune and Carlton. Actaea is a poeticus narcissi but a little later.

For forcing and greenhouse cultivation see page 129.

Polyanthus. Few of the early flowers can compare with the modern strains of this delightful subject in bringing colour and brightness into the house during the very early spring.

Polyanthuses must have a long season of growth and for early work the seed should be sown in February in mild heat. Prick out into trays or in the frame as soon as the seedlings can be handled. Plants for early flowering should be planted out as early as possible but as it is essential that the soil should not dry out during the summer and partial shade is necessary to avoid cheeks in growth, the plants must sometimes wait until early September before they can be put into their flowering quarters. In that case it is better to plant out closely together in a nursery bed where the needed conditions can be given and the final planting made as early in September as possible. Plant out on moist ground 6 to 8 in. apart.

Both frame and cloches are ideal for this crop. Two rows 9 in. apart can be planted under barn cloches and at 6 to 8 in. square in the frame. The plants will need coverage from late October to about mid-March and picking may begin as early as late January in the milder districts.

A highly fertile soil is needed if the plants are to give of their best. A good loam is ideal but in any case plenty of well decayed farmyard manure, leaf mould or well made compost should be dug in, plus a light dressing of a high grade complete fertiliser. A dressing of weathered soot seems to improve the colour of the flowers.

With so many really first class strains to be had only the best are worth growing and one of the Pacific strains should be chosen.

Stocks, Brompton. Early blooms of this fragrant and easily grown hardy biennial are always appreciated. The plants flower much earlier than the Ten-week varieties and produce a wealth of flowers from mid-April.

The seed is sown in May or early June in boxes and stood in a cold frame or sown in a seedbed outside. The seedlings should be pricked out at 4 in. apart into a nursery bed when large enough and transplanted to their flowering quarters in September, spacing the plants at 10 in. apart.

Cloches form a convenient method of protection and the plants should be covered in the late autumn or before any hard frosts occur. Decloche or give a larger cloche when the leaves reach the glass.

In the milder districts the plants can be decloched during March but a longer period of protection will encourage earlier flower production.

In milder districts the East Lothian strains can be grown either in frames or under cloches. The plant is smaller than the Brompton and the flowers are borne on shorter stems. These should be sown in July and planted at 9 in. apart in late September.

Sweet Peas. This is undoubtedly one of the most charming of all the annuals and deservedly popular in most gardens, not only for its beauty and fragrance but also for its long lasting quality as a cut flower. It is easy to grow but generous and careful treatment will give results that will repay in full measure the time and care bestowed on its cultivation.

Sweet peas gain by being sown in the autumn and overwintered under cold glass and sowings should be made during September in the north and in October in the south. A favourite method is to sow six seeds in a 5 in. pot. Good drainage is needed so well crock the pots and cover with coarse siftings and fill the pot with a good compost such as the J.I.P.1 or a similar mixture. Place the seed 1 in. deep round the pot and towards the rim. After watering place the pots in the frame and cover them with glass and hessian and slide the light on to the frame.

The temperature should be kept as even as possible until germination is first seen, when the glass and hessian must come off. When germination is complete give a little air by day but close the frame at night. After a few days the light can be left off during the day but replaced at night if the weather is cold. The idea is to encourage growth but without undue coddling. Give extra cover during a spell of frosty weather but well ventilate whenever possible.

Seeds can be sown in deep boxes and overwintered in the frame following the same routine as with the pots.

Planting out on the prepared site is done as early as possible in March but the condition of the soil and the weather must be the guide as to the exact time.

Spring sowing is convenient for those who cannot give the care and attention needed in overwintering, and sowings should be made in mid-February as described for autumn sowing. It is more usual to allow natural growth with the spring sown plants and they are allowed to climb and form a hedge which will be a feature of the garden and provide an abundance of blooms for cutting; but the finest flowers and stoutest stems will be had from the autumn sowings when grown on the cordon system and each plant reduced to one strong lateral. With the spring sowing the growing point of the main shoot should be pinched out at an early stage to encourage laterals.

A popular method for either autumn or spring sowing is to sow *in situ* under cloches. Autumn sowings are made in late September or early October. They will need cloching from early October until April. Spring sowings can be made during February or early March. The cloches will be needed until towards the middle of April. The young seedlings should be given some support by way of short twiggy stakes to prevent them falling over, and support given as soon as the cloches are removed. Where time is at a premium this method can be well recommended.

Tulips. As with narcissi and iris tulips need more height than many other subjects if they are to be given protection as they near maturity. With the frame this can be achieved by raising it in some way or by resting the lights on a temporary structure and draping hessian or polythene round the outside. Fig. 21 should make this plain.

Tulips are planted rather later than narcissi, the end of September or October is the time. The bulbs are planted closely together— the rows can be as close as 5 in. apart and the bulbs planted 3 in. apart in the rows. They should be planted 4 in. deep.

Cool conditions are needed until a good rooting system has formed so do not put lights over them until early December. Leaves will appear during January in the south and the beds should be carefully hoed through before the leaves tend to spread.

The earliest single tulips to do not produce sufficient length of stem to use as cut flowers and for decorative purposes these are better grown in bowls. The Triumph and Mendel tulips are the best for early cut flowers and varieties such as Krelage's Triumph, Van der Eerden, Weber, etc. are good varieties. The Darwins are a little later and have still longer stems and larger flowers. A number of varieties are excellent for cutting and Princess Elizabeth, Clara Butt, Rose Copeland and William Pitt are old and tried varieties. Golden Harvest is another favourite.

Cloches can also be used to produce early tulips and five rows can be planted under barns. As with frame work the bulbs should be planted at the end of September or during October, setting them at 3 in. apart in rows 4 in. apart.

As with frames do not cover until late November or early

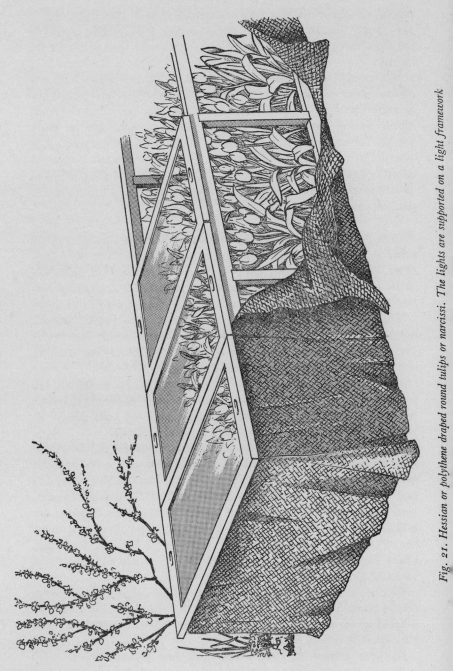

Fig. 21. Hessian or polythene draped round tulips or narcissi. The lights are supported on a light framework

December and as the flower stems lengthen substitute a tall type of cloche for a low one or raise in some way. Useful "elevators" can be had for this purpose (Fig. 12).

Violets. To obtain violets during the winter it is necessary to build up a good plant by the autumn and this can only be done if runners are planted out during April or early May, choosing if possible a showery period. The site should be fertile and dressed with plenty of organic matter. This will help towards maintaining the moist and cool root run that violets need.

For frame work prepare an area sufficient to allow the frame to be placed over the bed in the autumn and set the runners at from 12 to 15 in. apart and on no account allow the soil to dry out during the summer. Ample water should be given and the plants frequently syringed over with clear water. Cut off any runners that appear during the summer and give an occasional watering with soot water. A mulch of compost will be appreciated if given early in the summer (Fig. 22).

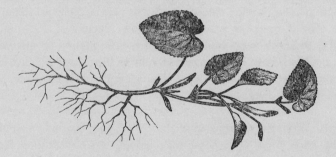

Fig. 22. A good type of violet runner

By September the plants should be well advanced and the frame must be placed over the site by the end of the month. Picking should be had from October onwards but bud formation will be slowed up during hard weather and every care should be taken to conserve warmth gained during the day by closing the frame early and giving extra covering during frosty weather, but ventilation must be given whenever possible.

Aphis and red spider can be a menace where violets are con-

cerned and appropriate methods of control must be taken as soon
as any trouble is noted.

For production under cloches treat as with frame cultivation.
Low barn cloches will accommodate two rows 10 in. apart, setting
the runners at intervals of 12 in. along the rows in staggered
positions. Cloche from September until March.

It is sometimes more convenient to transplant into frames early
in September. The plants must be lifted with a good ball of soil
and watered in. The frame should be kept closed for a few days
and shaded if necessary. Planting *in situ* is to be preferred.

Without scent a violet is a poor thing so select Princess of Wales.
Governor Herrick is a strong grower but is practically without
scent. Parma violets can be grown in frames in the milder districts
of the south-west or in a warm frame.

Wallflowers. A very early picking of wallflowers can be had from
either a deep frame or barn cloches. Lights or cloches should be in
position early in January. Normal sowings are made in the open
and the seedlings pricked out into a nursery bed. In September
the plants must be set out into their flowering quarters. Two rows
can be planted under cloches and the plants given a spacing of
8 in. Cloche or cover with lights during December. Plant out on
ground that has been well firmed and give plenty of ventilation.
The cloches should be removed as soon as the plants reach the top.

Good varieties for early work are Sutton's early Phoenix, Early
Flowering Fire King and Early Flowering Vulcan.

Zinnias. Amongst the many half-hardy annuals that can be cloched
in the early days with advantage zinnias are outstanding as cut
flowers. A native of Mexico they are seen at their best during a
sunny summer. That, of course, is a snag when growing zinnias
but cloches will help considerably in overcoming weather difficulties.
By being able to sow *in situ* and thus avoiding transplanting a
good healthy plant can be built up quickly and flowering had at an
early date.

The seed should be sown in a prepared bed at the end of March
or early April. Two rows are sown under barn cloches and the
seedlings thinned to stand at 6 in. apart. Seed can be sown in
mild heat in March in the greenhouse or frame and the seedlings
transplanted and covered with cloches towards the end of April,

but zinnias seem to resent transplanting and a bad check is often had and cropping suffers.

With direct sowing the plants will quickly grow away and will reach the top of the cloches during May. A taller cloche must then be used or a low pattern raised on elevators. It would be safe to decloche in late May but these sun loving plants will revel in the warmth under the cloches, and the longer they can be covered the better. Flowering will be had from early July until September.

Giant Dahlia-flowered is a popular type and splendid for cut flowers. It can be had in separate colours or mixed. There are also the Burpee Hybrids with curved petals similar to show chrysanthemums and a small type listed as Lilliputs.

SOME FURTHER USES FOR THE FRAME

Besides the production of vegetable and flower crops the frame has many other uses and by no means the least is that of providing the reserve space so often needed for greenhouse plants. It ensures suitable room for those plants that need cool but protected quarters during some period of growth and such subjects as primulas, cyclamen, cinerarias, freesias, winter cherry (solanum capsicastrum), calceolarias, etc. find in a suitably situated frame cooler conditions than would be had in the greenhouse during the summer. If high winds, rain or hail is threatened the lights can be slipped on and propped up at the back for the time being. Reference to these plants will be found in later chapters of this book. Space is also provided for those plants that have flowered and need a resting period.

PROPAGATION

The frame is also useful for propagating purposes and even in a cold frame successful plant raising can be carried out. For bedding plants the procedure in preparing the compost, sowing, pricking off, etc. is the same as described for the greenhouse (page 97), but in the case of an unheated frame the sowing date must be a little later, and a start is not advisable until towards the end of March with the half-hardy annuals, although a rather earlier start may be made with hardy annuals. Seedlings raised in the cold frame will not be ready quite so early as those raised in a heated house but they will be in good time for planting out in the summer borders. Indeed, a later sowing can sometimes be an advantage for so often the earlier sown seedlings must stand too long in the seed-boxes because the border is still occupied with the spring display. During the early days the frame must be kept as warm as possible and some extra covering in the shape of mats left ready to throw over the light if frost threatens, and warmth must be conserved by closing down early.

STARTING TUBERS AND CORMS

During late March begonia corms can be boxed up in damp peat and started into growth. If the frame is warmed the corms can be boxed up during February. When the shoots are 1½ in. long the corms must be carefully removed from the peat and potted into 3 in. pots and later into 5 or 6 in. pots (see page 178).

Dahlia tubers should be brought out of store towards the end of March and divided if necessary and boxed up in good garden soil. A deep box is needed so that the tubers can almost be covered, the soil being packed in between the roots with the fingers leaving the crowns exposed. The box must be watered and placed in the frame when growth will soon appear, and by planting out time they will be well ahead of those just brought out of store. An occasional syringing over will assist the growth to start. Frost must be kept out.

CUTTINGS

The frame is ideal for striking cuttings of many sorts both in the spring and summer, especially where soil warming conditions can be had. Many types of cuttings are taken during July, August and September. Geraniums, fuchsias, hydrangeas, heliotrope, coleus, calceolarias and many others will quickly root in the cold frame if struck in pots or boxes. A north facing frame is helpful at this time.

Chrysanthemum cuttings can be rooted in the frame, several cuttings being placed round 3 in. pots towards the end of February. Keep the frame closed until roots have formed or place the pots in a deep box in the frame and cover with glass. The frame can then be ventilated for the sake of other subjects occupying the frame at the same time.

For increasing the stock of dahlias cuttings can be taken when the shoots are some 3½ in. long. They should be severed with a sharp knife. The cutting is trimmed back to just below the bottom pair of leaves. Instead of trimming the cutting just below the bottom joint a small wedge-like piece of the tuber can be taken with the cutting to serve as a heel. As soon as the cuttings have rooted they should be potted up separately into 3 in. pots using J.I.P.1 or a similar mixture.

OVERWINTERING

One of the useful purposes the frame serves is in overwintering many subjects that might otherwise succumb to hard weather conditions. One subject in particular should be mentioned, viz. chrysanthemums. The stools are lifted after flowering, the old soil washed from the roots and the stools boxed in good garden soil. The boxes are placed in the cold frame and in the normal way brought into the warm greenhouse in January to encourage shoots to grow. They can be left in the frame if no greenhouse is available and cuttings taken and struck as soon as sufficient growth has been made. Pot up the rooted cuttings separately in 3 in. pots and keep in the frame until hardened off and ready for planting out (see page 111).

HARDENING OFF

Seedlings and cuttings raised under cover must be hardened off before being planted out in the open. This is even more essential when the plants have been raised in heat. The plants are transferred to the frame from the greenhouse and after a few days the hardening process can begin. This is simply a matter of gradually giving more and more ventilation by day and night until such time as the light can come off altogether during the day and eventually at night.

Some discretion is needed in this matter and weather conditions may make less ventilation advisable over certain periods in the early days.

7

The Greenhouse

The advantages of a greenhouse even where low coverage is extensively used is obvious and the serious gardener will soon feel the urge to build or purchase a glasshouse of some sort. Inside the house he will be able to pursue his hobby in comfort during the worst of weather and under appropriate conditions grow subjects that would otherwise be impossible.

Before committing oneself too deeply it should be realised that a greenhouse will make considerable demands on time and skill in cultivation if satisfactory results are to be had. Experience with cloche and frame cropping can be looked on as a very useful apprenticeship but unless one is prepared to devote the necessary time for the many demands that will be made it is better to leave the greenhouse alone. Nevertheless the enthusiast should not be put off because his or her experience of greenhouse work is scanty, for greenhouse technique can be acquired with practice. What must be clearly understood is that a greenhouse needs daily attention for plants need water, a constant change of air, feeding and keeping free of pests and disease. Tomorrow can be too late.

When thinking in terms of a greenhouse one should have a very clear idea as to the crops that are to be grown in it. What is the house to be used for? If the main purpose is to be the cultivation of pot plants a house with a fairly high base wall and fitted with permanent staging will be needed. On the other hand if the principal crop is to be carnations, tomatoes or chrysanthemums a house with ample head room will be necessary. Planting in this case can be carried out direct in the borders and chrysanthemums stood in pots on the ground. The base wall in this case would be a low one allowing the glass to come down much lower and giving more light over the borders. A house of this type with its higher roof will permit the buoyant atmosphere needed for such

plants to he maintained; but a house of this sort could be unneces-
sarily high and more expensive to heat than a plant house; nor
would it suit those plants needing a more humid atmosphere. In
most cases a varied collection of plants will be grown and it is here
that discretion is needed. A whole range of plants will quickly come
to mind that need, more or less, the same conditions as to
temperature, atmospheric moisture and ventilation and these can
be successfully grown together in one house. The list of plants in
chapter 17 will provide a guide as to general requirements. For a
general collection of pot plants a span-roof house with permanent
staging will be ideal.

Where a more varied selection of subjects calls for some different
arrangement there is no reason why one border should not be
cultivated and staging used on the opposite side. Several designs
are offered by manufacturers with glass to the ground on one side
and in such a house tomatoes, etc. are often grown with a collection
of plants, but all demanding somewhat similar growing conditions.

The glasshouse of today bears little resemblance to the glasshouse
of bygone days; the panes of glass are larger and supported on
glazing bars that are as light as possible consistent with the
required strength. Shortage of timber brought about the extensive
use of metal in the shape of iron, steel and aluminium alloys and
houses can be had in prefabricated sections ready for erection in
metal or wood. Metal houses have the advantage that the glazing
bars and framing are lighter than wood and there is even less
obstruction to light. Wood needs repainting every second year
with the exception of cedarwood which only needs an annual dressing with linseed oil. Aluminium alloys need no upkeep at all.

There are three main types of greenhouse used in private
gardens. The span roof type is the conventional and popular
greenhouse and without doubt the best where room and a suitable
site can be found. It is usually constructed on a brick, concrete or
wood base about 2 ft. 6 in. high but in some designs the glass is
carried almost to the ground. A span-roof house will permit a more
even distribution of light and the plants have the benefit of both
morning and afternoon sun. Air changes are more effectively
given by means of ventilators fitted on either side of the roof and
sides. Fig. 23.

The "lean-to" house is built against a wall facing south, south-
west or west—preferably south. It sometimes happens that a
position against an existing wall is the only available site or per-

Fig. 23. The span-roof greenhouse

haps the most convenient, but it must be realised that light will be directed from one side and that plants will tend to be drawn towards that side. The wall should be painted white so that as much light as possible is reflected. With care much good work can be done in a lean-to house if suitable staging is arranged and the plants well positioned (Fig. 24).

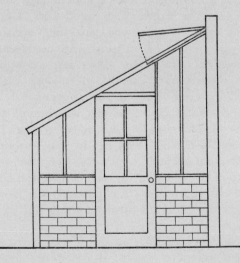

Fig. 24. The lean-to type of house built against a wall

Fig. 25. The three-quarter span house

The third type is known as a "three-quarter span". It is built against a wall the same as a lean-to but a lower wall will serve, the shorter side of the roof being built to rest on top of the wall. This type allows a more even and better distribution of light than in a lean-to and the useless sharp angle of wall and roof is eliminated. It is a better type than the lean-to but owing to the extra cost of construction it is seldom built now (Fig. 25).

Another design of house has become popular during the last twenty or thirty years. It is a span-roof type and known as a Dutch light house. This is based on the true Dutch light house where individual Dutch lights are built on to a structure during the summer. Houses of the Dutch light type differ from the true Dutch

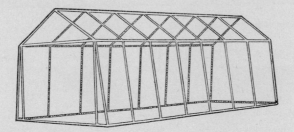

Fig. 26. A Dutch light house

light house in that they are constructed of large side and roof sections equal to four Dutch lights in size with glazed ends to fit the span shape of roof and sides. Most designs can be extended by adding fresh central sections. This type of house is really designed to allow crops to be planted direct in the borders but staging can be used and the house then forms a very good plant or general purpose house if heating is installed. Such a house can be very useful being approximately 12 ft. wide at the base and in sections of about 10 ft. long. It is one of the cheapest to buy (Fig. 26).

There are other types of houses but which will not concern the average amateur unless it is a case of taking over a garden with a greenhouse already *in situ*. There is the large commercial house of the vinery type used largely for tomatoes, carnations and crops needing plenty of ventilation. There is the aeroplane type where

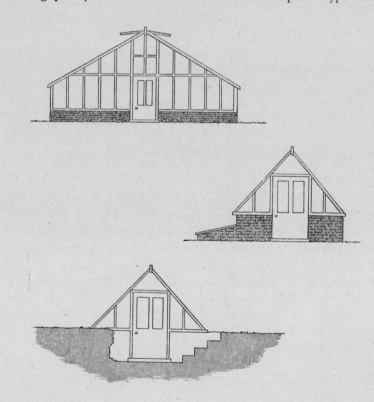

Fig. 27. Some other types of houses

a block of houses are built side by side thus saving the cost of inner walls, the valleys between the roof sections being supported on strong posts. A cucumber or forcing house is one in which the height of the glazed sides has been reduced so that nearly all the light enters through the roof. Such a house is often sunk into the ground. The object of the design is to conserve heat (Fig. 27).

THE SIZE OF A HOUSE

The size of a house must naturally be governed by the space available and the price the purchaser wishes to pay. Very small box-like structures are difficult to manage as they will be subject to extreme fluctuations of temperature and far too often equipped with inadequate ventilation. A late opening up on a Sunday morning in the spring or summer may find that the temperature has soared up into the nineties even in a fair-sized house and no plants will be happy under such conditions. A 10 ft. by 8 ft. house is very suited to the man with a small collection and the cost would not exceed by more than £10 or £12 than for a tiny 8 ft. by 6 ft. structure, and be far more useful and a joy to work in. A reasonable width is necessary for the smallest door will be 2 ft 6 in. wide thus leaving staging of 21 in. on either side and a central pathway of 2 ft. 6 in. in a 6 ft by 8 ft. house. If the width of the house is 8 ft. however, staging of 2 ft. 9 in. will be possible. In a house 12 ft. wide room is available for a central section of staging, which will add tremendously to the display.

VENTILATION

In buying a house see that adequate provision for ventilation is allowed for. This is vitally necessary to bring about the regular air changes needed to assist in maintaining the desired degree of humidity and temperature. Many small houses are not provided with sufficient ventilators but most manufacturers are only too willing to provide extra ventilation at a small extra cost and this is usually well worth while. Ventilators are placed in three positions —in the roof, in the sides and in the base wall under the staging. At least two roof ventilators should be provided, one on either side (Fig. 38 page 106).

THE SITE

The siting of a house requires some consideration, especially in smaller gardens and the most convenient position may not be the best. The site must be well drained for a badly drained site might be liable to flooding and in any case such a site would be a cold one and subject to excessive moisture in the atmosphere. Where such a site cannot be avoided it should be drained before the house is erected. A position opposite a gap between two dwelling houses through which wind will funnel should be avoided. This could cause considerable heat losses at times. Shelter is an advantage but avoid a spot likely to be overshadowed by nearby trees or houses. A site too near trees might result in broken glass due to a falling bough. As near as possible the house should run from north to south. This will allow a more equal distribution of light.

Do not suppose that the erection of a greenhouse will perform some miracle and turn bad soil into good. A bad soil will not be improved by covering. On the contrary, it will become worse for it will be deprived of the sweetening influence of frost, wind and rain.

HEATING

Space does not permit, nor is it intended in this book to give more than a brief guide as to heating the greenhouse. You will find a full account of this aspect of greenhouse planning in that excellent book *All About the Greenhouse* by A. J. Simons*. Heated greenhouses can be roughly placed into three main categories : (1) The cool house needing a minimum temperature of 40 to 50°F. (4 to 7°C.) which allows a wide range of plants to be grown. Such a house is economic to run and popular with many amateurs. (2) The temperature or intermediate house requiring a minimum temperature of 50°F. (10°C.) in which many of the plants grown in (1) would succeed and also many unusual and sub-tropical subjects. Quite obviously considerable overlapping will be had in these first two houses. (3) The hot or stove house; a house needing a minimum perature of 60 to 65°F. (16 to 18°C.) in which fascinating exotics can be accommodated and a range of tropical foliage plants. Such a house is, of course, expensive to run but a small part of a temperate house is often partitioned off and installed with extra pipe heat.

At the other end of the scale there is the cold house where only hardy subjects will be grown—especially alpines—or used to give protection to hardy plants but which might be damaged by severe

---

* *All About the Greenhouse,* A. J. Simons (Gifford).

outdoor conditions. A cold house or conservatory of any size would forward many flowering shrubs or the borders of a cold house would be ideal for early salads, etc. and from mid-April for tomatoes

Any method of heating must be reliable and capable of maintaining the desired temperature whatever the outdoor conditions may be. A good reserve is therefore needed in case of extra cold weather. There is still much to be said in favour of heating a small house by means of a solid fuel boiler and 4 in. pipes but a good deal of attention is needed in stoking and cleaning—often at inconvenient times. The fire area should be large enough to hold sufficient fuel to last the night through.

Small boilers are often designed to fit into one end of the house. Some protection from the weather is desirable, for stoking up from outside during heavy rain is no joke and some form of shelter should be contrived that is large enough to hold at least a small quantity of fuel. The boiler too will be all the better for being protected from the weather.

A modern method of heating is by way of electricity. Provided a temperature of not more than 45°F. (7°C.) is to be maintained the cost is not excessive and the chores of stoking and cleaning, etc. are avoided. Tubular heaters of the required wattage are used and can be thermostatically controlled—the heaters being switched on automatically when the temperature of the house drops below a predetermined level, and switched off when the desired temperature is again reached. For the busy man electricity—though apparently more expensive—can actually effect an economy in heating when time and convenience are taken into consideration and the saving in electricity which an accurate thermostat will bring about.

The electric fan heater has gained considerable popularity, especially for small houses. A fan drives warmed air round the house and both large and small models can be had. When, during certain weather conditions, only cool air is needed the fan can be used independently of the heater. Unlike tubular heaters these turbo heaters require no installation other than bringing in a mains supply to a switch and socket into which the heater is plugged. We have used these heaters for some considerable time and can thoroughly recommend them.

Electric immersion heaters may be employed either as a sole method of heating or to boost an existing boiler. Your local Electricity Board will glady give you particulars as to costs and work out for you the necessary wattage required to warm your house to the temperature required.

With large houses one of the fuel oil boilers will appeal on many counts. Such an installation can be completely automatic and a great time and labour saver. Fuel oil boilers are expensive to instal and for a small house they are not advisable. Boilers which utilise gas can also be installed or your solid fuel boiler adapted. Your Gas Board will advise you of suitable installations.

For a small house an efficient type of paraffin heater will prove useful. It will not provide a forcing temperature but it will keep out frost and in the normal way give a temperature of round about 40 to 45°F. (5 to 7°C.) A point to remember with such a heater is that it must be kept scrupulously clean and never allowed to smoke. A blue flame burner is recommended but it must always be borne in mind that a blue flame burner will consume more oxygen than a white flame and a chink of air should always be left on when the lamp is burning. A heater of this sort can also be useful as a means of boosting the heat from an existing boiler under extremely cold conditions.

Some excellent paraffin heaters can be had specially designed for greenhouse work, and there is no fear of harmful fumes from a modern blue flame heater so long as it is properly cleaned and adjusted.

During the colder months a lining of clear polythene will greatly help in reducing heat losses. One snag is that condensation is slow to clear and a certain amount of light is bound to be screened off; but if only the sides and lower parts of the roof are covered this is to some extent overcome. In any case care must be taken to fix the material in such a way that the ventilators can be operated. It is not so easy to fix the material to a metal framed house and it must be clipped in some way. The domestic clothes pegs will sometimes do the job quite well. Drawing pins will secure the polythene in a wooden framed house.

A difference of approximately 5°F. in temperature can be had by lining the house in this way.

In selecting and buying a new greenhouse make sure you are getting one that will be suitable for the crops you want to grow, and not merely because the price is right or the wife likes the look of it. The framing should be sufficiently strong to carry the weight of glass and be strong enough to stand up to severe weather. A reasonably rot-resistant wood should be chosen. Well painted deal is good but cedar is better and attractive in appearance. Oak and teak when treated are practically rot-proof but more expensive.

If a greenhouse has been taken over with the dwelling house one must accept it for what it is worth and make what improvements may seem necessary. A good clean down, the repair of any damaged woodwork and the re-glazing of any broken glass should be undertaken and the soil replaced or sterilised if the borders are to be used. Any heating arrangements must be checked before seriously getting to work with any cultivation and crops should be chosen for which the house would be most suitable.

8

Fittings and Equipment

It would be impossible to run a greenhouse without a certain amount of equipment and it may be helpful to mention here a few of the more essential items likely to be needed and often referred to in these pages, as well as some of the modern equipment that can be had.

POTS

A supply of pots, shallow pans and seed boxes will be one of the first essentials. These will of course be brought as they become necessary. The first requirements as regards pots will be for a number of 3 in. pots and 5 in. pots, for the majority of the plants will be flowered in 5 in. pots; but a few of the larger sizes will also be needed; some 6 in. and 8 in. pots as well as some of the larger 9 or 10 in. pots for such crops as chrysanthemums, tomatoes, etc. Pots must be looked on as being expendable, but with care in handling and storing the amount of breakages can be greatly reduced.

Clay pots have much to recommend themselves but they are expensive today and plastic pots have become very popular. They are less expensive and more easily cleaned than clays and do not dry out so quickly as a crock pot. Care must always be taken not to overwater them or the soil may become sour and airless. Pots made of bituminous paper, compressed peat, also fibre can be had, and where large pots for chrysanthemums are needed the bituminous kind are quite satisfactory, but they can only be used for one season. These can be had for 7d. or 8d. each at most garden centres.

New clay pots must be soaked in water for twenty four hours before being used.

SEED TRAYS

A few seed trays will be needed. A standard nursery tray will measure 14 in. by 8½ in. and may be from 2 to 3 in. deep. These can be bought at most garden centres. They will be needed for pricking out small plants or seed sowing. It may be of interest to know that one bushel of soil will fill nine trays 2 in. deep or six trays 3 in. deep. There is nothing special about these trays and similar ones can be made from boxwood. If the wood is treated with a wood preservative the trays will last a great deal longer. Use Cuprinal—never creosote.

POTTING BENCH

A potting bench of some sort is necessary, and where space is limited or a tool-cum-potting shed not available, a portable bench can easily be made and used at one end of the greenhouse bench, or

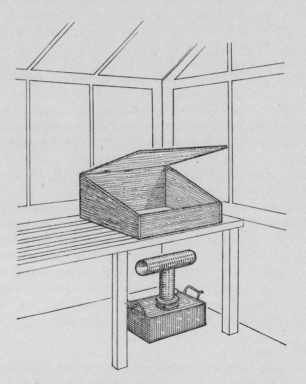

Fig. 28. A home-made propagating frame with oil heater to supply bottom heat, Dampened peat or sand should be placed in the floor of the frame

in some convenient shed and stored away when not in use (Figs. 21 and 22).

PROPAGATING FRAME

This is needed for the early germination of seeds; for growing on small seedlings and the rooting of cuttings. It can be a simple box of modest size covered with glass, but some means of providing bottom heat is necessary in the early days at least. This can be had by means of a small paraffin lamp or the box placed over the hot water pipes. Where the size of the frame warrants and electricity is available soil warming cables can be used (Fig.28).

Some very fine propagating frames complete with a plastic dome and thermostatically controlled heating can be had.

SOIL WARMING

A portion of the staging can be electrically warmed with advantage. A base of roofing felt or asbestos is first laid on the staging and boxed in with boards about 9 in. high. Cover the base with 2 in. of soft sand and on this lay the wires or cable. The wires should be covered with a further layer of sand or peat 3 in. deep and on this place the pots or boxes. A small frame placed on such a bed will form an excellent propagator. Damp peat packed between the trays or pots will help to conserve the warmth. The loading should be roughly $7\frac{1}{2}$ watts per square foot. It is usual to switch on the current at teatime and off again at breakfast time, thus giving a nightly dose.

AUTOMATIC VENTILATION

A fitting that will be appreciated by those who must leave the greenhouse unattended for a time is a simple device fixed on to a ventilator that automatically opens the ventilator when the temperature reaches a pre-determined height. The Humex Ventmaster is such a fitting and is non-electric. The device adjusts the vent according to the temperature changes both inside the house and outside. Electrically operated gear can be had but it is expensive and not a practical proposition for the small house.

THERMOMETERS

At least one thermometer should be in use and this should be of the maximum-minimum type for use inside the greenhouse. The tube is bent into the shape of a U so that there are two scales side by side. Inside the tube there are two metal pins which are pushed up by the mercury when it rises, and left behind when it recedes. The lower end of the pin in the left hand column marks the minimum temperature recorded, while that on the right the maximum temperature. The pins should be reset each morning by means of a small magnet supplied with the thermometer.

WATERING CANS

Two good watering cans are really needed even in a small house. The Haws type of can is ideal for greenhouse work and a convenient can would be a 3 quart as well as a 4 quart size. Tapered extensions are supplied to enable plants at a distance to be watered without damaging other plants. A fine and a coarser rose is needed.

SYRINGES

A syringe with a bent nozzle for getting a spray on to the undersides of the leaves should be had and one that will give either a fine mist-like spray or a coarse spray. The "Abol" is probably better known than any. Syringes can be had that give a continuous spray such as the "Mysto" and pneumatic sprayers are available for larger houses where a considerable amount of spraying will be needed.

DUSTERS

A distributor of some sort is needed to apply insecticides and fungicides in dust or powder form. One of the small bellows type can be had at a modest cost, but where a whole house is filled with the same type of plant, a blower is more effective and will discharge a cloud of dust over a large area.

MIST PROPAGATION

This is another modern aid for rooting cuttings under a regulated mist and in full light. The mist is automatically controlled by an "artificial leaf" placed amongst the cuttings. The "leaf" is subject to the same conditions of light and moisture as the leaves of the cuttings and loses moisture in the same proportion by evaporation. When the artificial leaf becomes dry a minute current of electricity is cut off and a magnet valve opens and allows mist to fall until a film of water again covers the "leaf" and cuttings. Soil warming cables provide bottom heat. Messrs. MacPenny supply a special unit for amateur needs. The complete installation will cost about

£20. It is a method that has proved highly successful where a very large number of cuttings have to be propagated.

EXTRACTOR FAN

When the greenhouse owner must be away for some hours an extractor fan is very worth while installing. The fan is fixed in the apex of the end wall of the greenhouse opposite the door. It is controlled by a thermostat which switches it on when the temperature reaches a certain height and switches it off again when the temperature falls. The thermostat can be set for any required temperature.

TOOLS AND SUNDRIES

Apart from the usual gardening tools the following should be at hand :

A good pocket knife.
Small secateurs.
A scrubbing brush with a good "wing" or one or two pot cleaning brushes (for 3 in. and 5 in. pots).
A stainless steel trowel.
A bin for rubbish.
A quantity of split bamboo canes for small plants and long thicker canes for tall growing plants.
A quantity of 4 in. labels.
Fillis and tying materials.

9

Greenhouse Cultivation and Management

It is only by careful cultivation and management that the green-house owner can hope to obtain the really first class show so much looked forward to. The aim must always be to create and maintain conditions as near as possible to those the plants would enjoy in their natural environment. This can only be achieved by watch-ful and painstaking attention to temperature, watering, humidity, ventilation and strict hygiene, and it is for this reason that plants grown together in a house must be reasonably similar in their their requirements. Fortunately most plants can adapt themselves to some extent to the conditions in which they find themselves, and a certain amount of latitude can be allowed.

STAGING

An essential part of the equipment of any house will be staging on which to stand the plants. This may be permanent or so arranged that it can be taken down and plants grown in the border. Staging supplied by the manufacturers is usually of slatted wood, the underlying idea being that air from the pipes or other warming system rises between the slats and past the pots. Many people prefer a staging of corrugated iron or cement-asbestos sheets covered with a layer of small shingle or weathered cinders. This can be kept dampened—a great advantage during warmer weather, and the pots do not dry out so quickly. Any staging should be firmly sup-ported and a narrow board nailed along the front to prevent the shingle spilling over. Shelving can be arranged at the eaves and supported by brackets, and if headroom permits a shelf can be suspended from the centre of the roof by means of specially shaped brackets. This, however, can put a heavy strain on the roof and only light pots should be placed there.

A lean-to house needs rather special staging. It is usual to fix staging along the front in the normal way and arrange tiered staging against the wall if room permits.

COMPOSTS

Before sowing any seeds or potting up plants we must have a suitable medium for them to grow in. It is even more important where greenhouse work is concerned than in the open garden that the soil in which our plants are to be grown should be suitable in every way, for the roots of plants in pots will be confined to the amount of soil in the pot. The soil must therefore be such that whilst being retentive of moisture it must be well drained and suited to the particular needs of the plant. Garden soil is seldom suitable in itself and a compost consisting largely of loam or good top-spit with sharp sand to keep it porous and open, plus fertilisers will form the basis of most mixtures.

We have to thank the work of Messrs. Lawrence and Newell of the John Innes Institute for a standardised compost that will suit most plants. When correctly made the mixture will be of the right physical condition and free of pests and harmful organisms. The loam must be sterilised before making the compost. A light compost will be needed for seed sowing and a stronger and more sustaining compost for pricking out and growing on.

For those who like to make their own compost the formulae are as follows:

The J.I. Seed Compost

2 parts medium loam
1 part peat } by bulk
1 part coarse sand

To this must be added:

$1\frac{1}{2}$ oz. superphosphate of lime
$\frac{3}{4}$ oz. ground limestone of chalk } per bushel

The J.I. Potting Compost No. 1

7 parts medium loam
3 parts peat } by bulk
2 parts coarse sand

To this must be added:

$\frac{3}{4}$ oz. ground limestone or chalk
4 oz. John Innes Base } per bushel

The formula for the J.I. Base is:

Hoof and Horn ($\frac{1}{8}$ grist) 2 parts ⎤
Superphosphate of lime   2 parts ⎬ by weight
Sulphate of potash   1 part ⎦

To make the J. I. Potting Compost No. 2 add 8 oz. base, and for the No. 3 add 12 oz. of base plus two or three times the quantity of chalk or ground limestone.

The John Innes Composts can be purchased ready to use from all garden centres and owing to the difficulty in obtaining loam this is often the only way of procuring a reliable compost. If you are lucky enough to be able to purchase good fibrous loam the opportunity should not be missed. Loamy turf from an old pasture should be stacked grass side down for six months. A thin layer of manure placed between the layers of turf will add to the value. The loam should be sterilised in some way but not the sand or the peat.

The difficulty in obtaining loam and the varying quality, to say nothing of the difficulty in sterilising, led to a new technique in composts in which peat and sand are used instead of loam.

These composts were evolved by the University of California and became known as the U.C. or soil-less composts. They need a different treatment to the standard loam composts and supplementary feeding must start sooner. Special care is needed to see that the compost never dries out or there will be great difficulty in re-wetting it. In fact, the only way seems to be to place the pot in water and allow the compost to absorb moisture until it is again moistened right through. It should not be compressed unduly when potting. Subsequent watering will do this and it should be nicely moist when used, but never sodden.

Soil-less composts can also be had from any garden centre, but for those wishing to make their own the following formula will be found satisfactory for general purposes.

Soil-less Seed Compost

Peat 50 per cent
Sand 50 per cent

To each bushel of this add:

Sulphate of ammonia $\frac{1}{2}$ oz.
Superphosphate   1 oz.
Sulphate of potash $\frac{3}{4}$ oz.
Ground limestone or chalk 4 oz.

Soil-less Potting Compost

Peat 50 per cent
Sand 50 per cent

To each bushel of this add:

Hoof and Horn	3 oz.
Ammonium nitrate	3 oz.
Superphosphate	2 oz.
Sulphate of potash	1 oz.
Ground limestone or chalk	4 oz.
Magnesium limestone	2 oz.

A compost of peat and sand will be less heavy than one of loam and easier to mix. Also it is cheaper. Once moistened it will retain the moisture longer than loam. Damping off seems to be less likely when using a soil-less compost and an extensive root system is formed in the early days. No sterilising is needed.

STERILISING

Loam should be sterilised before making the compost and also leaf-mould when this is used. The ideal method of sterilising is by passing steam through the soil and this is usually beyond the scope of the average amateur. Very small quantities can be dealt with by suspending a quantity of soil in sacking over a few inches of boiling water for three quarters of an hour.

Baking is a more practical way for any quantity and a simple way is to raise a sheet of iron on some bricks and build a fire under it. The soil should be broken down and in a damp condition and placed on the iron sheet. It should then be covered over with a wet sack. The fire under the iron should be distributed over as wide an area as possible. With a slow fire it will take about two hours to bring the soil to a temperature of 180 to 200°F. (82 to 93°C.) when it can be allowed to cool. Take care not to overbake the soil or let it become dry or the texture will be ruined. The temperature should be checked with a thermometer from time to time. Really large quantities are dealt with in specially designed sterilisers. A well known make is the Sterilatum made by Messrs. Attwood & Jones of Stourbridge.

Chemical sterilisation is effected by means of formaldehyde or cresylic acid. Formaldehyde is more generally used and is applied as a 2 per cent solution, i.e. 1 gallon of formaldehyde to 49

Hyacinths grown in pots or bowls make an attractive show in the early part of the year. The variety here is Princess Margaret – a light pink.

Naegelia. These plants which need warm treatment give a grand display in the later summer and autumn. The long tubular flowers of vivid scarlet add a welcome splash of colour.

A well grown bowl of Paper White narcissi.

Cockscomb (Celosia cristata). A beautiful and showy plant that bears brightly coloured flowers like a crest or cockscomb.

Fuchsia. Favourite and popular plant needing only cool treatment. Many lovely varieties are listed.

Freesias from both seeds or corms make delightful pot plants as well as being ideal for cutting.

gallons of water. The soil should be spread on a clean hard path or a cement floor that has first been watered with the solution. Spread the soil out to a depth of 3 or 4 in. and apply the solution via a fine rose. Two gallons are needed to each bushel of soil. After treating throw the soil into a heap and cover for a week to retain the fumes. The cover can then come off and the soil given a few turns to release any fumes. If the heap is left outdoors it should be protected from the weather. The soil will be ready to use in a month or five weeks.

After taking all this trouble to sterilise take care that the soil remains uncontaminated. A dirty floor, or a dirty shovel or barrow can re-infect the heap and render the whole work useless.

Another convenient method of sterilising is by electricity. Moist soil is packed between two electrodes. The resistance offered by the soil to the current causes heating, and the soil is removed when the temperature reaches 180°F. (82°C.) or just over.

Although we speak of sterilising it should be remembered that only partial sterilisation is brought about. If it were complete the useful, as well as the harmful bacteria would be destroyed, and the soil would be useless for gardening. Partial sterilising will destroy disease spores, eggs, insects and weed seeds.

PROPAGATION

A start will be made by purchasing a number of plants to furnish the greenhouse but if a continuity of cropping is to be had fresh plants will have to be raised both from stock and from seed. Half the fun in running a greenhouse lies in raising one's own favourite plants and a sense of achievement can justifiably be felt when a successful batch of plants is produced.

There are a number of ways in which plants can be propagated, the more usual method being by means of seeds or cuttings. Many plants are increased by offsets or divisions, others by layering and some by leaf cuttings. Reference will be made as to the best method of propagation in the list of plants in Chapter 17.

SOWING AND PRICKING OFF

Many of the seeds likely to be sown will often need rather more warmth than will be had on the open staging. It is here that the propagator described in Chapter 8 becomes so useful, the extra heat being localised.

A light and open compost similar to the J.I. Seed Compost must

4—GUG * *

be used for the tender threadlike roots must be able to penetrate easily into the soil. The compost should neither be too wet or too dry. Seeds are sown in pots, pans or shallow boxes. Whichever is used must be clean and the pans or pots crocked to ensure drainage. A little coarse fibre sieved from the peat should be used to cover the crocks and prevent fine soil from running through. The prepared compost is now placed over the fibre and lightly firmed. The surface should be level. Water via a fine rose if necessary and stand to drain.

Most of the seeds will be small, some in fact very small and should be evenly scattered over the surface of the compost. The essential thing is to sow very thinly so that the resulting seedlings will have room to develop, otherwise they will become weak and attenuated from the very start. Small seeds need only the lightest of covering; the finest need no covering at all but should be merely pressed into contact with the soil.

After sowing cover the container with glass and brown paper for seeds germinate better in darkness and the glass will conserve moisture. It should be turned daily to allow condensation to be cleared. Remove the paper as soon as germination is seen and the glass within a day or two. Many gardeners now simply slide the containers into a polythene bag. If water is needed before germination is complete, or while the seedlings are still very small, the container should be immersed almost to the rim in water so that the water will seep up from the bottom to moisten the compost right through.

The seedlings will need to be moved into a stronger compost as soon as they can be safely handled. Where only a few seedlings are needed a pan does very well and individual seedlings are often pricked out into 3 in. pots, but for larger numbers a standard seed tray is called for.

A compost such as the J.I.P.1 or a similar mixture should be used and after placing coarse siftings or a little dampened peat in the pan to cover drainage holes the pan or pot is filled with the compost and lightly firmed. Subsequent watering will consolidate the soil and the seedlings. When dealing with a seed tray some roughage must first be placed along the bottom and the compost added. This should be lightly and evenly firmed by pressing it down with the fingers and taking special care of the corners and sides. A little more compost will then be needed and this should be pressed level with a firming board, leaving the surface $\frac{1}{4}$ to $\frac{1}{2}$ in. below

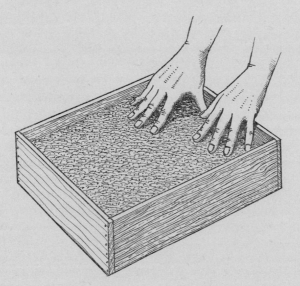

Fig. 29. Pressing the soil in the seed tray with the fingers. See that the sides and corners are not neglected

the top of the tray. Water with a fine rose and stand to drain. (Fig. 29).

We are now ready to prick out the seedlings. First remove a number from the seed pan with an old table fork, taking care not to damage the roots. The space given the seedlings will depend on how quickly they are likely to develop and how long they are to stay in the tray or pan. The usual spacing is roughly 2 in. and 3 in. for the larger kinds. A standard tray will hold forty-eight seedlings, i.e. six rows of eight. Use a short blunt dibber to make the hole and holding the seedling by one seed-leaf lower it well into the hole and then draw it up until the seed-leaves are just clear of the soil. A slight pressure with the dibber leaves the seedling firm (Figs. 30, 31 and 32).

CUTTINGS

Many of the plants grown in the greenhouse are increased from cuttings and the propagating frame or warmed bench becomes almost a necessity, as a close and moist atmosphere is needed with an appropriate temperature. The soil in which the cuttings are placed must be sandy and for some subjects sharp sand only is

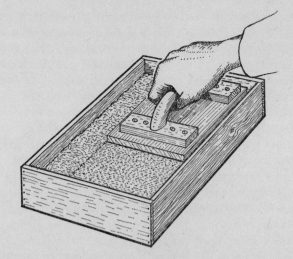

Fig. 30. Firming and levelling off the compost previous to sowing or pricking out

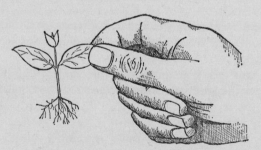

Fig. 31. Hold a seedling by one of the seed-leaves when pricking out

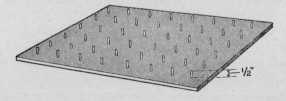

Fig. 32. A template a shade smaller than the inside of the standard seed tray with 48 pegs of ¼ in. dowelling appropriately placed will ensure a neat job of pricking off

used. Any medium used must be capable of holding moisture but must also be well drained. The J.I. Seed Compost is suitable for many cuttings and where bottom heat is used, vermiculite and peat in equal quantities or sharp sand and peat is ideal, but as these materials contain no plant food once rooting has taken place the cutting must be given a move into a normal compost.

A favourite method is to place several cuttings round the edge of a 3½ in. pot. A 3½ in. pot will take four average sized cuttings. When taking the cuttings select shoots which are actively growing. These root more quickly than short hard cuttings, for although cuttings may be soft or half ripe or hard and woody it is with the soft or half ripe cuttings we shall be more concerned with for greenhouse work. Fuchsias, chrysanthemums, geraniums, etc. are typical.

When preparing the cutting remove as few leaves as possible but enough of the shoot must be had to ensure firm insertion. The base of the cutting must be trimmed at a point immediately below a node or joint and it is important to use a very sharp knife or razor blade. A good clean cut is needed or the base of the cutting may rot. A hormone rooting powder such as Seradix will help towards good rooting. The base of the cutting is merely dipped into the powder before inserting. Do not insert the cutting too deeply (Fig. 33).

The pots are plunged up to the rims in the moist peat of the propagator or stood on a soil-warmed bench. The lid of the

Fig. 33. A prepared cutting. Always use a sharp knife or razor blade and make a clean cut just below a joint

propagator should be closed. This is done to maintain a moist
atmosphere and reduce the rate of transpiration. The rooting
medium must be kept moist and the cuttings syringed over daily
and shaded. When the odd few cuttings are taken the pot can be
stood in one of a larger size containing moist peat. With a piece
of glass placed over the top it forms an improvised propagator.
Another method is to enclose the 3½ in. pot in a plastic bag closing
the mouth with a clip or tie. A short cane will keep the cuttings
clear of the bag. During the spring and summer many cuttings can
be struck on the open staging without bottom heat but they should
be covered with polythene (Figs. 34 and 35).

The time taken for cuttings to root will vary according to kinds
and methods. Cuttings struck in vermiculite and peat or sand
and peat will root very quickly; those rooted in a mixture of loam,
peat and sand more slowly. With the latter however there will
not be the urgent need to move them into a stronger compost.

Instead of cuttings it is often possible to propagate by means of
leaves. Various plants including gloxinias, begonias, saintpaulia
and streptocarpus are readily increased by leaf cuttings. A healthy
and well developed leaf is taken and the stem cut off to within
half an inch of the leaf, and the stem and base of the leaf are

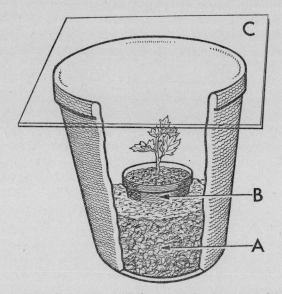

*Fig. 34. An improvised propagator. (A) damp peat placed in a 5 or 6 in. pot, (B) a
cutting in a small pot. (C) glass to conserve moisture*

Fig. 35. An odd cutting or two can be placed in a pot enclosed in a polythene bag. A thin cane or two will hold the bag away from the cuttings

inserted in a similar compost to cuttings. Roots form where stem and leaf meet and in time several little plantlets appear at this point. Another way is to take the leaf and lay it underside down on the surface of a suitable compost. A cut is made on the under-side through the principle mid-ribs at the junction of a pair of ribs. Several cuts can be made on a large leaf. If the leaf is held down by bent wire or even a few pebbles a callus will form at the cuts and tiny plants will form. These methods need bottom heat and a temperature of 65°F. The compost must be kept moist for the least dryness will cause the leaf to wither (Figs. 36 and 37).

Many plants are increased by division. Ferns, orchids, bamboos, aspidestras, greenhouse grasses, etc. Old plants can be divided up into two or more sections and planted up separately. Care must be taken not to treat the plants too roughly and to endeavour to tease out the roots after removing all the old dry soil. Although some plants can be divided at any time the spring is the best time to do so when the plant is ready to start a fresh season of growth.

One of the most important tasks in the greenhouse is that of pot-ting and unless this work is carried out with skill and understand-ing the plants cannot thrive. Growing plants demand conditions suitable to their size and wellbeing, and repotting is done when the

Fig. 36. Propagation by means of leaf cuttings (Saintpaulia). The stem is trimmed to ½ in. and the stem and ½ in. of the leaf is inserted in the cutting compost and placed in a propagating frame with bottom heat

roots are running well round the insides of the pots and before the plants become what is known as pot bound. Small plants, however, should not be potted direct into large pots but rather in progressive moves as growth dictates.

Always use clean pots. To use a dirty pot will completely negative any sterilising that has been done and furthermore roots will hang on to the sides of a dirty pot and prevent the ball of soil sliding out easily and resulting in damaged roots. Old pots should therefore be well scrubbed inside and out and stored away ready for use —a job that can be done at any odd time.

Fig. 37. Another method of propagating from leaves. (Begonia, etc.) The veins on the underside are almost severed and then placed right side up on the moist compost and pinned down. The compost is a mixture of peat and sand. The leaf must be placed in a propagating frame and given bottom heat

Drainage is highly important. When drainage is impaired the soil in the pot will soon become sour and water-logged and the roots will suffer. A few crocks should therefore be placed over the drainage hole although where small seedlings or cuttings are being dealt with a little peat or coarse fibre will serve. Larger pots must have a large crock placed over the hole, convex side uppermost, and a few smaller crocks over and around this. A little coarse fibre should be added to prevent any clogging of the drainage system through the fine soil being washed between the crocks.

After seeing that the pot is well drained place a little compost in the pot and with a seed label lift the small plants from the box into which they had been pricked out. The little plant should be held with one hand at the correct depth and compost trickled in round the plant with the other. A tap on the bench with the pot will settle the compost and leave the plant fairly firm. Subsequent watering will consolidate both soil and plant. With these smaller pots leave $\frac{1}{4}$ in. below the rim for watering.

Repotting into larger pots follows somewhat the same procedure but the larger the pot the more crocks will be needed. The plant should be well watered before turning it out of the old pot. To remove the plant support it by placing the fingers on either side of the stem and turn the pot upside down and give one or two sharp taps on the edge of the bench. The plant will then slide out and be held safely in the hand. Remove any old crocks from the ball.

A little soil must first be placed in the bottom of the pot and the plant stood on this making sure that it is at the right depth. It may be necessary to remove or add a little more compost to arrive at the right depth, bearing in mind that with a bigger pot from $\frac{1}{2}$ to 1 in. must be left for watering. See that the plant is in a central position and trickle in the soil all round. Firm with the fingers—not with the thumbs—or a rammer. Do not ram too hard for few plants need such treatment. When extra firm potting is needed as with chrysanthemums it will be mentioned when dealing with such plants. What is necessary is that the compost should be evenly consolidated so that no air cavities are left.

VENTILATION

Reference has already been made to this important matter in the previous chapter but some further notes are appropriate in this section for success or failure will depend a great deal on the intelligent use of the ventilating system. Fig. 38 shows an effective ventilation system and it will be seen that under such conditions a constant change of air will be had.

Extra care must be used when giving ventilation or the plants will be subject to direct draught. Normally side vents would only be used during the summer and then at some risk of wind changes. The box or under stage ventilators would be far safer and it is a pity they are not seen more often in modern greenhouses.

Ventilation should always be given on a rising temperature and lessened as the temperature falls. As a general rule ventilators are

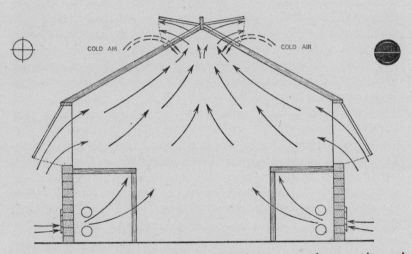

COLD AIR

COLD AIR

Fig. 38. An ideal method of ventilation. Fresh air passes over the warm pipes and rises. Side vents should only be used during warm and still weather. Two roof ventilators are needed; that on the windward side being closed as needed to reduce the intake of cold air

opened in the morning and closed or partially closed at night to conserve the warmth. Roof vents are opened first in the morning to remove stale air and assist circulation. The extent to which they are opened must be governed by the weather. Side vents will be opened later. What is important to remember is that ventilators should be opened on the lee side of the house except when the air outside is still. It should never be necessary to have to rush in and open up everything to cool the house down. If you want an extra hour or two in bed on a Sunday morning in the summer an electric extraction fan will take care of things.

WATERING

The question is always asked "How often should I water a particular plant?" and the answer "when the plant needs it" is not very helpful but true. So much will depend on weather conditions, type of compost, the season and the kind of plant. In general both overwatering and underwatering can be disastrous and to say that a plant will need watering once a day or once a week would be misleading.

A growing plant must never be too wet or too dry. A plant will need watering when the roots have absorbed the available moisture in the compost. Sufficient water must then be given to moisten the compost right through. During hot and sunny weather it may well be that further watering will be needed that evening or next morning, for much of the moisture taken up by the roots will be lost by excessive transpiration as well as by other causes. Under dull and wet conditions another watering would only tend to make the compost sodden and a continuance of this treatment would result in a sour and airless compost with inevitable root troubles.

A plant should never be left to dry out so that the compost shrinks away from the side of the pot. In this case water will run down between pot and soil and very little will have a chance to get into the compost. If this should happen the pot should be stood in water for a time until the compost has again taken up its full charge of moisture. In general most plants will need ample water during the spring and summer when they are actively growing but in the autumn and winter the supply must be considerably lessened and dormant plants kept more or less dry. During the autumn and winter any watering should be done early in the day.

When watering always direct the jet carefully against the inside of the pot and fill the space left for that purpose. It is often necessary to lift the foliage to do this. A test as to whether the soil is well moistened is to rap the outside of the pot with a "rapper". If the pot gives off a ringing note the soil is dry but a well moistened pot will give off a dull note. Needless to say it is no good rapping a plastic pot.

For the sake of convenience alone it is advisable to have a water tank in the greenhouse. If rain water from the roof can be run into this so much the better so long as an over-flow is provided. A neglected and dirty tank, however, can be a very real source of disease and it should be emptied and well cleaned at intervals.

SHADING

Light is essential to all plants and during the darker days when light is frequently below the requirements of most plants it is vital that no light should be excluded.

There are times, however, from early April onwards when bright sunshine directed through the glass can be a source of danger. In the early days this may happen for brief periods only, but long enough to cause damage, especially where seedlings are concerned and unduly high temperature rises. Some temporary shade must be contrived and blinds or old muslin curtains will do the job.

Later on in the late spring and through the summer more permanent shading can be applied to the outside of the glass. Limewash, starch and whiting or one of the proprietary shading compounds such as Summer Cloud can be used just sufficiently thick to break the direct rays of the sun. The disadvantage of shading in this way is that it is permanent and must remain whatever the weather may be. Exterior blinds of wood laths can be had; they are expensive but can also be used during the winter to help hold off frost. Blinds of plastic material can be had for interior fitting and these too provide shade just when it is wanted and, like the exterior blinds, can be rolled up to admit full light during less sunny weather.

FEEDING

It would be most convenient if all the nutrients a plant will need during the season could be supplied at the beginning. Unfortunately this cannot be done for it would be rather like giving the baby steak and kidney pudding because he will need it later.

The plant food that can be given in a small amount of compost is insufficient to feed the plant for all time and as growth and flowering make demands on the food supply there comes a time when the limited supply fails and supplementary feeding must be done or growth and development will be held up. Frequent watering will tend to leach out supplies, especially nitrogen, and intensify the shortage. What is known as a feed is therefore given at regular intervals preferably in liquid form and which will contain a balanced proportion of nitrogen, phosphate and potash in accordance with the needs of the plants. Cucumbers for instance will need a feed that is high in nitrogen and tomatoes one that contains a high potash content.

Concentrated proprietary liquid feeds can be had to suit all classes of plants and these can be relied on to supplement the food supply. They should be used strictly in accordance with the makers' instructions and need only diluting.

STAKING AND TYING

A great many greenhouse plants will need supporting in some way if the display is to be effective but care must always be taken to make any support as inconspicuous as possible. Chinese split bamboo canes dyed green are largely used and can be had in lengths from 18 to 30 in. Unfortunately these are now in very short supply. Large bamboo canes will be required for chrysanthemums and taller growing subjects.

For tying, raffia or bass is used and should be soaked in water before using. Soft three-ply fillis is a favourable material for tying in. Another very convenient method of tying is by way of a flexible green strip 4 in. long with soft wire running through it. A twist secures the tie. The trade name is "Twist-It". Suggestions as to training and tying will be found where necessary in the list of plants in Chapter 17.

10

Chrysanthemums

When the amateur gardener first acquires a greenhouse his thoughts in many cases turn to chrysanthemums for the autumn and winter. As a start he sets out to provide cut flowers for the home and a display in his greenhouse. Later he may decide to grow flowers and plants for exhibition. It is, however, not the object of this book to go into the finer points of growing chrysanthemums for exhibition, but to tell the reader how they can be grown to provide a supply of flower from October to January.

There is a tremendous range of colour, shapes and sizes and a range of varieties can be chosen so that flower is available over a long period. Each variety has a natural flowering time which can only be altered artificially (see section on A.Y.R. chrysanthemums) and catalogues generally give the flowering time of a variety, its colour, shape and height. The main shapes grown for cut flowers are exhibition incurved, reflex decorative and intermediate decorative. Reflex blooms have petals which all curl outwards and downward from the centre; intermediate blooms have outer petals which reflex and inner ones which curl over the centre; incurved blooms have all petals curving inwards so as to form a ball when petals are fully formed. In addition to these some singles are grown for cut flower and many spray varieties generally listed as American Sprays. If the reader is interested in the classification of varieties, and if he shows chrysanthemums he must be, we would recommend him to join the National Chrysanthemum Society which publish many useful books for the chrysanthemum grower.

STARTING A COLLECTION

The best way to begin is to study a range of catalogues and to make a selection of varieties to suit your personal taste. If possible visit chrysanthemum shows so that you see the finished product of some varieties and this may help you to make a selection. You would then receive the young plants in March and April. On receipt they should be potted into 3 or 4 in. pots and a suitable compost for this potting is J.I.P.1. For a few days the plants should be kept shaded in the greenhouse and given an occasional damping over on sunny days. When established the shading can be gradually lifted and the plants will grow on. In early April pots should be transferred to a cold frame but choose weather conditions which are not too cold as the young chrysanthemum plant is very susceptible to cold damage. When established in the cold frame ventilation should be given on an increasing scale until by the end of April the glass is only put on at nights when frost is imminent.

POTTING ON

As these small pots become full of roots the plants must be moved to a larger size and a 5 or 6 in. pot should then be used. J.I.P.2 is a suitable mixture to use but remember to place a crock over the drainage hole in the pot. When these pots become full of root in late May or June the plants should be moved on into the final pot, i.e. the one in which the plant will flower. This should be a pot of 9 in. diameter and these days it is usual to use 9 in. red bituminous pots for this final potting. This type of pot is much lighter and very much cheaper than crock pots, and although it can only be used once, the advantages outweigh the replacement costs. The compost used for this final potting can be J.I.P.3 or 4 though some prefer a compost which is a little stronger than the John Innes mixture and in this case a little extra loam is used. It is not necessary to pass the loam through a sieve but is best chopped down from the stack with a spade so that the mixture is a little "nutty" in texture. This final potting should be done leaving the soil surface about 2 to 3 in. below the top of the pot to allow for top dressing later in the season. It is usual to use a pot rammer in order to make the compost very firm.

SUMMER STANDING GROUND

When the plants leave the frame they must be stood throughout the summer on a site that will allow full sunshine. The ideal standing ground is one with an ash base. Concrete is not very good as it tends to become too hot and if bare earth is used excessive rooting into the soil may result. Each pot should have a 4 ft. cane beside the plant and as the plant grows it is tied to this cane. The top of the cane should be tied to a horizontal wire about 3 ft. 6 in. above ground level support when plants become large and possibly top heavy later in the season there is a danger that they may blow over in wet, windy weather (Fig. 39). The site can be kept clear of weed by the use of Paraquat weedkillers. Boards to keep the sun off the pots can be used and if you have to use a concrete standing ground then we would suggest that the concrete be first covered with a layer of peat or straw and the plants stood on this. Throughout the season the plants must be watered, never overdoing it, but you may find that in the late summer on hot sunny days they may sometimes require watering twice a day.

FEEDING

In the early stages sufficient plant food will be available from the compost but after the final pot is full of root, feeding should start and it will be difficult to improve on proprietary chrysanth-

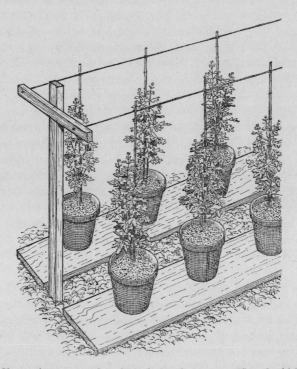

Fig. 39. Chrysanthemums stood outdoors during the summer. They should be stood on an ash base or on boards and well secured against wind

emum feeds though with experience you learn the effect of certain feeds and the appearance of the plant when it is in need. Generally early in its life one feeds for steady maintained growth but as flower buds develop then more potash is given to encourage quality and flower colour intensity. During this late Summer period it is usual to apply another inch or so of compost to the final pot. This encourages fresh surface roots which respond rapidly to subsequent fertiliser applications.

STOPPING

Stopping is the removal of the terminal inch or so of growth on any shoot. As a young chrysanthemum plant grows it will eventually terminate in a flower bud. This is known as the natural break bud. A first stop anticipates this bud and directs growth into laterals. These laterals terminate in what is called a first crown bud and it is these buds which provide the blooms for show work. A second stop anticipates this first crown bud and when given again produces a multiplication of laterals. Most American Sprays and late November and December varieties are given two stops and the second crown buds allowed to develop—see list of varieties (Figs. 40, 41 and 42).

DISBUDDING

Disbudding should not be confused with stopping. As already explained stopping is the process whereby the growing point is removed; disbudding is the process of removing the competing side buds around a terminal flower bud to produce a large bloom. Many growers may not wish to do this but will leave each shoot and its buds to develop naturally without disbudding. In this case the terminal flower will be a little smaller but two or three other flowers will be opening around it when the main bud is fully open—a spray.

HOUSING

In late September the plants must be carried into the greenhouse and stood there until they produce flower. Before carrying in the plants one or two obvious practises should be followed. Pots should be clear of weed and any diseased or damaged leaves should be removed. It is a wise plan to give the plants a fungicidal and insecticidal spray so that they go in clean. They can be laid on their sides for this spraying. Remember they will still grow in the greenhouse

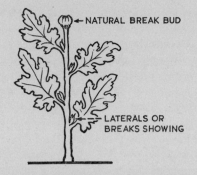

Fig. 40. Stopping chrysanthemums. Natural break

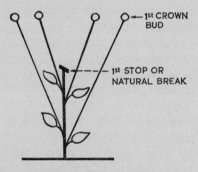

Fig. 41, Stopping chrysanthemums. First stop or natural break resulting in first crown buds

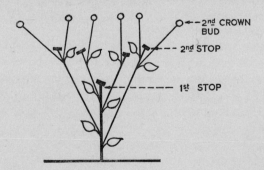

Fig. 42. Stopping chrysanthemums. Second stop resulting in second crown buds

and so sufficient room should be allowed not only to get to the plants to disbud but so that the air can move freely around the plants. As much ventilation as possible should be given until the weather limits the amount the ventilators can be open. Eventually flowers will be formed and as flower buds open and the weather deteriorates a time is approached when all your skill will be needed to produce the perfect finished product. Air must be kept dry and buoyant and in many instances it may be necessary to have a little heat on and yet still have roof ventilators open. A damp stagnant atmosphere is fatal at this period. A fan heater is ideal as it just warms the air and keeps it moving rapidly, but make sure any fan heater is not positioned so that the plants are in direct line. It is important when watering housed plants that it be done early in the day so that any excess moisture has dried off before nightfall. A temperature of 50°F. (10°C.) is ideal.

LIFTING

In order to save trouble some gardeners plant their greenhouse chrysanthemums in the garden for the summer months. This certainly saves potting and watering but they must still be taken into a greenhouse during the latter part of September. They have to be lifted and replanted in the greenhouse border then well watered in. The removal is facilitated if about a week before they are to be lifted a spade is used to cut around each plant, pushing the spade down five or six inches away from the plant all the way round. This severs some roots and new roots are formed within the circle. Wire baskets can also be sunk in the garden and the plants put in these. This makes the job of lifting into the greenhouse much easier but the quality of the flower grown by this method is not usually quite as good as the methods set out above.

STOOL TREATMENT AND PROPAGATION

After flowering the plants should be cut down to within 6 or 8 in. of the soil level and the stools knocked out of the pots and the soil carefully removed. Wash off the roots and replant the stools in boxes 3 or 4 in. deep. Stools can be fairly close together but make sure they are all labelled. A potting compost should be used and the stools kept a little on the dry side. They should also be cool and not in any great warmth as they should have a resting season. In late December, January or February according to variety and your facilities the boxes of stools should be placed in a warmer situation and given a little more water, when the stools will soon produce new growth. Watch out for greenfly at this period as the soft new shoots are very susceptible to attack. As these cuttings reach a length of 2 to 3 in. they can be detached and rooted to make new plants. Cuttings should be made with a straight cut across the stem immediately below a node and the bottom leaf removed. They can be rooted using soft wood cutting techniques in a mixture of peat and sand, sand, or J.I. Cutting Compost. Cuttings taken in January will root with very little covering but those taken the end of March will require polythene covering to the frame and some shading. If your propagating frame withing the greenhouse is equipped with soil warming cables then rooting will take place in 10 to 15 days. An air temperature of 50°F. (10°C.) is sufficient for cutting production and propagation. When rooted the cuttings should be potted off as described earlier. It is usual to root large exhibition and incurved varieties in early January and the others during February and March. However, perfectly good flowers can still be produced if, because of your local conditions, cuttings cannot be taken until April.

VARIETIES

The choice of varieties has to be so much a matter of personal taste that we hesitate to give you any sort of a list, but would certainly suggest that for November flowering varieties you visit chrysanthemum shows and make a list in conjunction with the catalogues available. Those varieties which flower in early and late December cannot however often be seen at shows and so we would offer a few suggestions. For mid-December Mayford Perfection and its colour sports in red, bronze, yellow, etc. is exceptionally good and is one of the easier families to grow. It should be given two stops with the second early in August. The Shoesmith Salmon family can also be very highly recommended. It has many colour sports and constitutes the main supply in shops at Christmas time. Give this family two stops, the second at the end of July. American Beauty is a first class white and the Favourite family is also a useful family to grow. Again two stops, the second in late July. American Sprays are extremely popular and a selection should be grown.

SPECIMEN PLANTS

Sometimes very large plants are seen bearing upwards of 100

flowers and these large plants make a magnificent show. One of the
best varieties for this is the Princess Anne family and in order to
produce the best plants early rooting of cuttings is essential. Cultivation is as described before though they may finish in a larger pot,
but stopping is varied so as to produce many more breaks. The first
stop is given as soon as the plant is 6 to 7 in. high. A second stop
follows when laterals have reached a length of 6 or 7 in. and so on
and it is possible to give as many as five stops, but the last stop
must be done by the end of July or early August, as otherwise there
will be very little stem. With careful staking and trying using a wire
frame a plant two to three feet in diameter can be produced with
the flower heads all at approximately the same height. Other
varieties grown in pots are the Charms and Cascade. These can be
grown from seed sown in mid February and the seedling pricked off
until they finish in a 5 or 6 in. pot. The Charm will branch
naturally and produce a decorative plant perhaps 18 in. high and
up to 2 ft. in diameter without having been stopped but allowed to
grow and branch naturally. Flowers are single somewhat like stars.
Cascades require similar treatment but as the plant hangs out over
the pot the pots have to be kept up on a stand and the shoots can
be tied in to a frame hanging below the pot. Both these varieties will
flower in a cold greenhouse.

COMMERCIAL METHODS

During the last decade the professional chrysanthemum grower
has realised that the long term method of growing chrysanthemums
in pots is an uneconomical one because of the labour involved,
though usually he will admit that it produced first class flowers. A
method has been evolved which is known as "direct planting".
Rooted cuttings are purchased in June and July and are planted 6,
8 or 9 in. apart straight into the greenhouse border. When the
plants are established and growing one stop is given in early August
and according to time of planting and distance three or four shoots
are allowed to develop. Disbudding follows in due course. Where
greenhouses are not available until August the grower will often
plant two or three cutting in a 9 in. pot during June or July and
give one stop in late July, taking the plants into the greenhouse as
space becomes available. These chrysanthemums and those planted
direct in the ground are usually supported with a wire and string
framework or a specially made welded wire mesh of 6 or 8 in. hole
width.

ALL THE YEAR ROUND CHRYSANTHEMUMS

It has been found that by artificially controlling day length chrysanthemums can be made to flower at any period of the year. The technique is to extend the day length by artificial lighting in the winter months in order to encourage growth and then to allow the plants to flower. Without the extended day length premature flower bud would result. In summer or long days it is necessary to use 100 per cent black shading to create an artificially longer night in order to make the plants produce flower bud. Throughout the technique closely controlled growing conditions must be used as this is really a form of precision growing. Tables are available which give details for each week of the year of the amount of light required and the length of shading necessary for any particular variety, though not all varieties are suitable for this process.

DWARF POT CHRYSANTHEMUMS

For most of the year a similar light and shade technique is used to produce the dwarfed pot chrysanthemums which are available as pot plants. Princess Anne and family and Woking Scarlet are the main varieties used for this work. Rooted cuttings are obtained and several planted around a five in. pot. The plants are kept short by spraying them with the dwarfing compound ß-nine now available to the amateur. Very few amateurs have the equipment to produce these pot chrysanthemums other than during the autumn and early winter months but he can do it at this period of the year without light or shade control. Rooted cuttings are planted around the edge of a five in. pot in late September using J.I.P.2 or 3. In ten or fourteen days when the cuttings are established and growing a soft pinch is given and three or four laterals allowed to develop. These produce flower in December and January if a temperature of about 50°F. (10°C.) is maintained. The plants stay dwarf just as those which are seen in the shops. It is worth noting that any cuttings taken from these dwarfed plants would revert to their normal height and flowering date the following year.

Cuttings can be obtained in summer from specialist growers or your old stools will continue to produce if fed and shoots kept cut back till the cuttings are wanted. Spring rooted cuttings can also be kept cut back if grown in a frame to produce cuttings in July, August and September.

11

Fuchsias, pelargoniums and Hanging Baskets

It is convenient to deal with these subjects in one chapter as fuchsias and pelargoniums have many features in common and are often used as the meaty part of hanging baskets. Both fuchsias and pelargoniums are extremely popular plants, not only for pots but for the garden. Societies exist for enthusiastic growers of these subjects and their aims include encouragement to novices and the spread of information and often specialist shows are arranged.

Pelargoniums and fuchsias are attractive as pot plants and many growers use them for the bulk of their summer flower display in the greenhouse. They are fairly easy to grow and will give a wealth of flower over a very long period. Some of the Irene varieties of zonal pelargoniums are quite good for winter flowering but a minimum of 50°F. (10°C.) is needed to keep them actively growing and flowering. The greatest use for them however is outdoors during the summer months.

Pelargoniums are not hardy, though some of the tougher specimens stay out of doors during the winter in the coastal strips along our south and west seaboard, but even then damage may occur in very hard winters. Fuchsias are a little hardier than pelargoniums and will often shoot from below ground even when the top has been killed by frost. Deep planting with fuchsias and the provision of protection in the form of autumn leaves, peat, bracken, etc. will often allow varieties like Tenessee Waltz or White Spider to be left out during the winter. Some varieties of fuchsias are much hardier and include the species magellanica or the variety Alice Hoffman, etc.

Propagation of both pelargoniums and fuchsias is by soft wood cuttings. These can be rooted in a mixture of peat and sand or other cutting compost. In August and September they will root happily in a north frame, but in autumn or in spring a propagating case with a little bottom heat situated in a greenhouse should be used. When rooted cuttings should be potted off into 3 in. pots using a compost such as J.I.P.1. Give a little shading, particularly with the fuchsias, until the plants are growing away and then with the careful application of warmth and water keep them growing steadily. In winter they will not require a great deal of moisture, in fact with geraniums the moisture must be related to temperature and light conditions. Stopping must be done in order to produce a bushy plant and in both cases it should be done when the plant has made some 5 or 6 in. growth. In this first potting it is not necessary to crock, but a little peat can be placed in the bottom of the pot. When the 3 in. pot is full of root, they should be moved into 5 in. pots and the best specimens eventually moved to a 6 in. or even a 7 in. pot, but this may not be necessary until the second year. Over-potting geraniums must be avoided as it will tend to produce an over foliaged plant. When plants are established for the summer in their flowering pots, the occasional use of a liquid fertiliser will keep the plants in growth and encourage further flower bud formation.

PLANTING OUT

Geraniums, which is the common name for zonal pelargoniums, are frequently used for bedding out in flower beds or in window boxes and for this purpose a late autumn struck cutting or even early spring cutting taken from stock plants overwintered in a warm house, provide the ideal short bushy plant which is wanted for this work. The soil should not be on the rich side and the geraniums should be given a sunny position. Strong semi-shaded positions may tend to make a very soft spreading plant which makes growth rather than flower. This is especially so in the American Irene varieties as these, a naturally vigorous family, will often run riot in any situation where the roots are not restricted. With these varieties it is quite a good plan to plant out leaving the plant still in the pot. Fuchsias on the other hand require a good rich soil and one with good moisture holding powers. A position where some shade occurs during the daytime is very useful but they will succeed in full sun providing they are given extra water and occasionally damped over.

WINTER CARE

For most of the country if you wish to retain your geranium plants they must be lifted and kept protected during the winter. This can be done by boxing them up in September or October, giving them one watering and then allowing the soil to become almost dry. Keep them in a greenhouse or other light and airy situation with a minimum night temperature of 40 to 50°F. (5 to 7°C.). If you wish to take cuttings from these plants during the late autumn or early spring then the plants lifted should be potted and cuttings taken from them as they grow during the winter. For this a higher temperature would be required, about 50°F. (10°C.). Fuchsias which have been planted out can also be lifted and boxed and allowed to rest during the winter in the same conditions as indicated above for geraniums. Standards must be brought in as otherwise the stem part could easily be killed.

PELARGONIUMS

Under this family name we have a great variation in types and it includes the Regal and Show pelargoniums, the Zonal pelargoniums usually called geraniums, miniature and scented leaf varieties, Ivy geraniums and one or two other small groups. Regal and Show pelargoniums are usually grown in 5 to 6 in. pots and allowed to flower during the summer months in the greenhouse. It is possible to use the American variety Grand Slam and similar ones as bedding plants during the summer. This is because these varieties are shorter than the older varieties and have a much longer flowering period. Traditionally cuttings of Regals are taken during July from plants which have flowered and been cut back. Subsequent growth provides the cuttings. However with the American varieties cuttings can be taken at other times, in fact whenever there is vegetative growth and the right conditions for rooting can be given.

In the authors' opinion the greatest introduction in Zonal pelargoniums in recent times has been the Irene geraniums. There are about sixty varieties though many are rather similar and it would be better to leave it to the gardener to choose a collection of varieties that appeal to him.

It has been the practice of some gardeners to raise Zonal geraniums from seed. They would not come into flower very quickly and of course there has been great variation in habit and flower. New varieties, unless they are sports, must be raised from seed and the amateur, and professional too, can get a lot of fun by cross pollinating geraniums and raising plants from seed. But up to recent times one never knew what the results would be.

However a new F.1 hybrid type has been bred and given the name of "Carefree" Geraniums. At the present seed is available in ten varieties in shades of pink, crimson, salmon, picotee, scarlet, red and white. Seed has been scarified and should give nearly 100 per cent germination. The seed should be sown in January and plants should be ready for bedding out in June, and they will come into flower soon after. No pinching is required and the hybrid vigour produces a bushy plant which blooms profusely until frost comes along. Because of their free flowering bushy habits they are particularly suitable for window boxes and other similar situations.

IVY GERANIUMS

Used largely for hanging baskets and in such positions where they can be tied to walls or allowed to hang down. In the early stages it is advisable to use an 18 in. cane to each plant and to tie in the breaks as they grow, as otherwise plants become tangled and many shoots will be broken in moving them.

FUCHSIAS

Fuchsia cuttings can be smaller than pelargoniums but like them nodal cuttings are best, though it is said that fuchsias will root quite well from internodal cuttings. The main necessity is one pair of fully expanded leaves plus sufficient stem to insert in the rooting media. We have said earlier on that young plants must be pinched to induce bushiness and sometimes a second and even a third stop is necessary in order to obtain a well furnished plant. During the summer when fuchsias are being pot grown for display it is worth remembering that from pruning to flowering takes about six weeks so if you want a particular plant for a show then cut back flowering shoots about six weeks in advance of the show, and it should again be in full bloom for the show. When growing standards the cutting should not be stopped but the main single shoot allowed to grow on, supporting the stem by tying it to a cane. Stop this shoot at the height at which you wish the standard to flower.

After fuchsias have had their winter rest in pots then they can be started into growth by plunging the pots in water to soak the ball of soil and roots and as soon as young growth starts they should be repotted by removing much of the old soil and potting into a

similar or even smaller size pot. Standards should be pruned back
to the head at this stage.

HANGING BASKETS

The use of baskets hanging in places where they can be seen
to advantage is becoming more and more widespread, possibly
due in part to the Britain in Bloom Campaign. A well designed and
balanced basket carefully planted and tended gives months of
colour. Choose plants with a long flowering season, using types that
will succeed in the selected position, e.g. geraniums for full sun,
fuchsias for partial shade, etc. When hanging the basket don't
aim at putting it up as high as possible, as much of the beauty can
be missed; try and have a basket hung at about—or just above—
eye level, but watch your head. Remember baskets can not only be
hung outdoors but will add to the charm of the greenhouse if hung
from the purlins or roof bars, and these will continue to flower
long after those outside have finished. Ferns and other foliage
plants such as Chlorophytum and Tradescantia can be used to give
a nice winter effect in the warm greenhouse.

PLANTS TO USE

We have already mentioned several, and below are a few others,
though it must be remembered that it is not comprehensive, and
much variation can be achieved with a little imagination :

Ageratum. A short annual with small powder puff flowers in blue
which has a very long season of flowers. It can be raised in a warm
house by seed sown very shallowly in February.

Asparagus. The so-called asparagus fern, *A. Sprengeri*, is a very
useful plant for basket work. Its long trails are most effective. Two
plants, one on either side, will be sufficient. The smaller, *A.
Plumosus nana*, can also be used.

Begonia. The best varieties to use in a basket are the pendula
type, though the large flowered ones can be used putting two or
three to each basket. Corms should be started into growth in
February and March and transferred to the basket when planting.

Impatiens. This plant you may know as the Busy Lizzie and the
new F.1 hybrid Imp makes an ideal subject for a basket as it will

flower continuously until frost comes. Usually raised from seed in February or March and discarded at the end of the season.

Lobelia. Though the ordinary dwarf varieties of lobelia can be used the normal one for basket work is the trailing or basket Lobelia. It can be raised as a half-hardy annual sown during February. It is often a good plan to plant a few basket Lobelia through the moss in the basket, siting them about half way up the basket. Six to nine plants should be used in each basket if this method is adopted.

Marguerite. This white daisy like flower can be used to advantage in the confined soil conditions of a hanging basket. It should be raised from cuttings taken from stock plants overwintered in a cool house. At most two plants would be required in a basket.

Nasturtium. This annual can be introduced into a basket by placing a few seeds in the right place when filling up the basket. Thin to leave only three or four per basket.

Petunia. This is a very good plant in a basket and we particularly like the F.1 hybrid grandiflora. Raise plants by sowing in the warm house in February or early March.

FILLING AND PLANTING

You will find that unless some support is given to the basket when filling and planting it tends to roll away from you, thus making the operation difficult. We find that a ten inch pot or a pail standing on the potting bench with the basket stood in the open top forms an ideal support. The chains can be disconnected or allowed to hang down at the side. In order to keep the compost in, the basket must be lined and it is traditional to do this with moss or thin turves—grass side outwards. Green polythene can be used but looks a little unsightly until hanging plants fall well down outside the basket. It does however prevent the compost drying out too quickly, but remember to make a few holes in the bottom in order to allow for drainage. When the lining is carefully placed in position then compost can be put inside, carefully firming it as you go. Make sure the moss or other lining is not displaced or the soil will wash out at the first watering. Don't fill quite to the top but place your proposed plants in position and finally fill to bring the level about an inch below the top wire of the basket. Compost used can be J.I.P.2 or 3 but remember that as many plants will be expected to grow in a small amount of soil, feeding in the form of liquid fertiliser will have to be given at ten to fourteen day intervals in order to maintain the plants in good condition. Always try and make up your basket during the latter part of April so that it can hang in the greenhouse for a fortnight or three weeks during which time the plants will establish themselves. Choose favourable conditions before taking out and hanging up the basket. If necessary it may have to be hardened off as one would half-hardy annuals.

During the summer watering will have to be done and the best way is to unhang the basket and place it in a tray of water, leaving it there until the soil surface shows wet. Then drain and rehang.

12

Winter and Spring Colour in the Greenhouse

In the greenhouse autumn merges imperceptably into a winter that bears little relation to outdoor conditions. Many plants will still be gay with flowers when frost has laid its icy fingers on those growing in the open. Spring too, comes so much earlier in the warmth and shelter of the greenhouse that flowers associated with the spring can be enjoyed while winter is still with us.

Many gardeners rely almost entirely on a show of chrysanthemums to provide colour during the late autumn and early winter, and what a riot of colour they provide; but it is sometimes overlooked that the beauty of many other subjects can also be enjoyed at this time, and that a very extensive choice of plants is available. Fuchsias, geraniums, coleus, and many other plants associated with a summer display will continue to give colour over a long period during the darker days. There are as well a large number of plants that will continue the succession of flowering during the winter and the early months of the year.

Here are a few of the more popular subjects recommended for winter and early spring work in the greenhouse and which can be grown with little trouble if a minimum temperature of 45°F. (7°C.) can be maintained and rising to 50 to 55°F. (10 to 13°C.) during the day. Slightly lower temperatures will still produce good results in most cases, but flowering will be somewhat later.

Azalea. Azaleas are hard-wooded plants and belong to the genus Rhododendron. Several species are suitable for a greenhouse display and make a magnificent show of bloom from December until May. The most popular species is *A. indica.* It is an evergreen and the earliest to flower.

Young plants of the so-called Indian or *A. indica* should be purchased from a nurseryman in the early autumn when they should be full of buds. The plants should first be stood in water for an hour or two and then potted. Good drainage is needed and a compost of three-quarters peat and a quarter loam is recommended, plus enough sharp sand to keep the mixture open. Do not add lime. Firm potting is necessary.

When potted the plants should be stood in a well lighted spot. Frequent syringing over with clear water will encourage growth. Do not over-water but see that the compost is kept moist. A liquid feed given occasionally will help the buds to swell.

After flowering and as the weather becomes warmer the plants should be stood outdoors. Pick off dead flowers as soon as the plant ceases to flower and place outdoors in full sunshine. Here the plants can stand until early October. It is an advantage to plunge the pots in ashes to ensure cool and moist root conditions during the summer. After flowering the plants can be repotted if necessary, using only a slightly larger pot. Frequent syringing during the summer will encourage growth and help to keep down red spider.

Azalea indica is chiefly increased by grafting but it can be propagated by means of half ripened cuttings taken during the late spring. Insert the cuttings in sharp sand and peat and place them in a propagator with a little bottom heat. Rooting is slow and somewhat uncertain.

Begonia. One of the most showy and popular plants for the winter months is the fibrous begonia Gloire de Lorraine. It grows to a height of 18 to 24 in. and has roundish light-green leaves and terminal clusters of delicate rose-pink flowers.

Propagation is by means of cuttings and basal shoots are taken during March or April and finally potted on into 5 or 7 in. pots in a compost of equal parts loam and leafmould or peat. A little well decayed manure and a quantity of sharp sand should be added. A moist and semi-shaded position is needed with a minimum temperature of 50°F. (10°C.). The slender stems must be given support by way of thin canes and any flower buds removed until October, when they should be allowed to develop. Weak manure water or a liquid feed should be given weekly from this time.

After flowering the plant should be cut half way down and very little water given until February or early March and the plant then restarted into active growth to provide basal shoots for cuttings. Other winter flowering begonias are *evansiana*, a Chinese autumn flowering pink, and *fuchsioides* a scarlet which grows to a height of some 5 to 6 ft.

Begonia semperflorens is better known as a summer bedding plant but provides a charming pot plant for the late autumn when sown in late June or July. Cuttings can be taken from older plants and root easily at this time. Organdy—a F.1 hybrid—is vastly superior to the older open-pollinated varieties. Galaxy is another F.1 hybrid.

Begonia rex and its varieties are grown for their foliage. They made a colourful show during the winter, and a few plants on the staging will add greatly to the general interest. Propagation is carried out by means of leaf cuttings or by seed sown during March or April.

BOUVARDIA

Dwarf greenhouse flowering shrubs hailing from South America. They have slender stems with small leaves and bear clusters of red, pink or white flowers during the late autumn and winter. The flowers are tube-like opening out at the ends into four petals.

Young plants are raised from cuttings taken in the spring. The old plants are cut back in February after flowering. They should be well watered and the foliage syringed over frequently to encourage new shoots. These are taken when they are 2 in. long with a heel and inserted into pots of sandy soil and placed in a propogating case with bottom heat. When rooted pot up separately into 3 in. pots using the J.I.P.1 or a similar mixture. When established pinch out the growing point and treat any side shoots similarly to encourage a branching habit. The plants whould be potted on into 5 in. pots and placed in a cool frame until mid-September when they can be brought into the greenhouse where they will continue to flower well into the winter.

BULBS

Bulbs in pots or bowls make an appreciable contribution to the greenhouse display, especially during the early weeks of the year. Most are easy to grow and do not need any great heat. They are particularly useful as they do not take up valuable space over long periods of growth and are accommodated in a plunge bed or in a frame for the greater part of their lives. A few pots of narcissi, tulips or hyacinths will provide a wealth of colour and interest in the greenhouse from Christmas until May if small batches are

piglossis makes excellent pot plants.
d should be sown in July or August
e plants are to flower in the spring.
magnificent specimen once seen
Chelsea will be remembered.

Where sufficient warmth and suitable
conditions are available. Dracenas
will add colour and interest to the
general display. Dracena sanderiana
is one of the most colourful.

rous-rooted begonias make attractive and colourful pot plants. Modern Fl hybrids
as the new Muse Rose are compact and produce a brilliant display over a long period.

Capsicum "Fips" – a new introduction. The deep red fruits are borne well above the leaves. The plant provides colour during the dark days.

Dwarf beans. Showing method staking when plants are grown in under glass.

A group of house plants will make an attractive addition to the greenhouse display as well as being available for the dwelling house.

planted at varying dates and brought into the greenhouse at intervals of a week or two.

Narcissi. The narcissi family includes bulbs commonly known as daffodils and narcissi—the trumpet types usually being referred to as daffodils. They flower in their natural habitat in early spring but flowering can be advanced by weeks in the greenhouse.

It is well to remember that unless a good flowering size bulb is planted, no matter how good the compost or how well they are cultivated, the results will be disappointing. The ideal narcissi bulb for pots is a double-nose bulb which will give two good blooms. The actual size will depend on the variety but cheap and under-size bulbs will not pay for the trouble taken where pot culture is concerned.

For the earliest flowers the bulbs should be planted during August. The J.I.P.2 can be used or a mixture of good garden topspit, leafmould or peat and sharp sand to which a liberal sprinkling of bone meal has been added. One of the soil-less mixtures can be used where loam cannot be had.

A large pot should be used for root room is too restricted in small pots. A 6 in. pot is needed to accommodate three or four bulbs. The tips of the bulbs should be well seen when the pot is filled to within 1 in. of the rim. In a 7 in. or 8 in. pot a wonderful and lasting effect is had by planting in two tiers.

When bowls without drainage are to be used bulb fibre must be used instead of a compost. This can be had from all garden shops ready to use or can easily be made by the user. It consists of six parts by bulk of peat, two parts of crushed oyster shell and one part charcoal. The fibre must be well wetted and drained before use.

After planting the pots should be watered and stood on an ash base in a cool and shady place. A spot under a north facing wall would be ideal. The pots or bowls should be covered with 5 or 6 in. of fine ashes, peat or sand. A thick covering of straw is sometimes used.

The bulbs must stay in this plunge bed for some eight weeks. This is to ensure cool and moist conditions while a good root system is formed. In about eight weeks the pale young leaves will be coming through the neck of the bulb and about 2 in. high, when the first of the pots can be taken into the greenhouse.

Do not subject the bulbs to any great heat at first and keep them well shaded until the leaves become green, when full light can be given and rather more warmth allowed. Do not over-water but see that the soil is kept moist. A day temperature of 50°F. (10°C.) is sufficient. As the leaves and flower stems lengthen some support will be needed.

After flowering the pots can be stood in the frame or in a sheltered spot outside to allow the leaves to feed back into the bulbs as they die down, and when the bulbs are harvested and cleaned they can be planted in the open garden for outdoor flowering the next spring.

The smaller flowered narcissi such as Dove Wings, Peeping Tom and the hooped petticoat types make delightful pans or bowls. Small chips placed over the surface of the pans will enhance the effect and improve conditions.

It is quite possible to have daffodils by Christmas if prepared bulbs are planted. These bulbs will have first been given warm treatment to complete formation of the flower within the bulb, followed by a cooling treatment. This ensures rapid growth when the bulb is planted. When prepared bulbs are purchased it is essential that they should have been kept cool and not exposed to warm conditions in shop or store or the treatment will be rendered ineffective.

Early flowering varieties should be chosen. Paper White and Soleil d'Or will be amongst the first to flower and these can be followed by such well known trumpets as Golden Harvest, Carlton, Magnificence; Fortune is also a favourite for early work. Actaea is a popular Poeticus, but rather later.

Where flowers may be needed for early cutting the bulbs can be planted closely together in a box 4 or 5 in. deep and partly filled with good garden soil. The bulbs are placed almost touching and pressed into the soil. Further soil is added and well firmed by pressing it down between and round the bulbs until only the tips are exposed. The box is then well watered and plunged in the normal way. The box should be taken into the greenhouse during September for forcing in the same way as described for pots.

Hyacinths. Hyacinths are seen in the shops from just before Christmas and through the winter. They can be had quite well in the amateur's greenhouse at a very early date if prepared bulbs are planted in good time. Bulbs of 16 cm. size will give the best flowers and these are potted up as for narcissi in August and September.

For really good specimens one bulb to a 5 in. pot is enough and where two or three are grouped together a larger container must be used.

Plant with the nose of the bulb well showing and after planting and firming water well and plunge as described for narcissi, but do not leave in the plunge bed quite so long as you would narcissi.

When taken from the plunge bed into the greenhouse keep in a darkened place for a time. A partially darkened space under the staging (but not too near the pipes) is a good place. When growth becomes green full light can be given.

Do not mix the colours in one pot or bowl. Growth may be very uneven—one colour often becoming fully out while another is still a fairly tight bud. Support will be needed by way of a thin cane.

Roman and Italian hyacinths are the first to bloom and are treated in the same way as other hyacinths.

After flowering allow the bulbs to finish off in the frame and in due course plant them in the open.

Tulips. These are dealt with in much the same way as narcissi but putting up can be left until September or October. Unless flowers are needed for cutting for indoor decoration pots or bowls of the earlier kinds are more acceptable than the taller and later varieties.

The earliest to flower will be the Duc van Thol type. These are the short-stemmed types seen in quantities in the florists' shops at Christmas time. Brilliant Star and Couleur Cardinal are examples. These are followed by what are known as "Earlies"—i.e. Keizerskroon, Bellona, Prince of Austria, etc. These have longer stems and make most attractive pots. Next there are the Mendel and Triumph varieties—not quite so early but invaluable for a spring display in the greenhouse.

The Duc van Thol kinds should be potted up in August and plunged until November. "Earlies" are potted in September and Mendels and Triumphs in early October. Four bulbs can be grown in 5 in. pots. Any open potting soil will serve or fibre where bowls are used. In that case the size of the bowl must, of course, determine the number that can be accommodated.

The pots or bowls should be left in the plunge bed until they are full of roots and the top growth an inch or two long. Keep them darkened for a week and leave them in the frame. If one or two pots are taken into the greenhouse each week a succession of flowering will be maintained.

Once tulips are well rooted they will stand a fairish amount of heat for ordinary purposes a temperature of 50 to 55°F. (10 to 13°C.) is sufficient and at this temperature the blooms will last longer. Aphides are very liable to attack the young growth of tulips and a strict watch should be kept for any signs of this pest or the blooms will be damaged.

Prepared tulip bulbs can be purchased and will bloom at an early date.

Cineraria. No flowering plant is of greater value to the owner of a greenhouse during the early days of the year than the many varieties of cinerarias. It is deservedly one of the most popular of greenhouse plants and with a little management will give a brilliant display from December until April.

There are several types grown. *C. grandiflora* is the best known and grows to a height of 15 to 18 in. It bears large single flowers. *C. stellata* is a large plant with branching heads and small star-like flowers. Then there are the dwarf multiflora strains which grow to a height of 12 in. and carry a mass of blooms. Such strains as the Hansa or *multiflora nana* are ideal where space has to be considered but at the same time produce a mass of colour.

For an extended display two or three sowings should be made. Sowings made in mid-April will flower in December. The main sowing is usually made in early June to provide a display in January and February and a July sowing will extend the season into March and April. Most amateur gardeners will, however, rely on an early June sowing for a general display in the early part of the year. Cultivation is not difficult but it is a subject that resents neglect and prefers cool conditions.

The seeds are very small and should be sown in pans filled with finely sifted compost. This must be watered before sowing. Sow the seed over the levelled surface of the pan and sift over the merest covering. Cover with glass and paper or push into a polythene bag and stand in the warmest part of the house. Once germination is seen remove the paper and give a little air and remove the glass in a day or two but continue to keep the tiny seedlings shaded

When the seedling are large enough to handle pot them up separately into small pots or prick them out into a seed tray 2 in. apart using J.I.P.1. The next move should be into 3½ in. pots and as soon as they become established move them out from the house and place in a cool frame shaded from bright sunlight. During the summer give ample ventilation and only put the light over in case of heavy rain or cold winds; but always keep shaded from strong sun and make sure that the pots do not dry out. Another shift should be made when the pots become full of roots and the plants repotted into 5 in. pots. After repotting leave the light over for a few days but give a little ventilation. The frame can then come right off and only be replaced during inclement weather.

During October the plants must be taken into the house, but previously pot on into 6 or 7 in. pots any that show extra vigour. The smaller plants can be flowered in the 5 in. pots quite well. As soon as the flower stems start to push up a weekly liquid feed should be given and this can alternate with soot water. Feeding should cease when the flowers open but take care to keep the soil in the pots just moist. Over-watering will quickly bring about the collapse of the plants.

The secret of success with cinerarias is to keep them cool and for that reason they are ideal for a cool house. Watch out for aphis and leafminer and take steps to deal with these pests as soon as seen. Frequent syringing over with clear water and occasionally with an insecticide will do much to prevent any trouble.

Cyclamen. The Persian cyclamen is one of the most important of the winter and spring greenhouse flowers. The plants can be raised either by sowing the seeds or by planting the dried corms or tubers. Of the two methods the first is to be preferred.

Seed should be sown in August in pans containing a compost such as the J.I. Seed Compost. It is usual to space the seed about $1\frac{1}{2}$ to 2 in. apart and cover with 1 in. of sandy compost. The seed germinates slowly and irregularly and needs a temperature of 55 to 60°F. (13 to 16°C.). Sowing at $1\frac{1}{2}$ in. square allows a quickly germinating seedling to be removed without disturbing others.

When the seedlings are $\frac{3}{4}$ in. high they must be pricked off into seed trays containing a light compost and grown on in a temperature of 55°F. (13°C.). By early spring they will have made three or four leaves and should then be potted on separately in 3 in. pots using the J.I.P.2 or a similar mixture. When planted the tiny corm should be just visible at soil level.

In June the seedlings are given a final potting into 5 in. pots using the J.I.P.3. A little well rotted manure that has been rubbed through a coarse sieve can be added to the compost with advantage. Take care at this stage not to bury the corm entirely. Once established the pots can be stood outdoors in a cool frame. Keep the frame well ventilated and lightly shaded. A north facing frame is useful for this crop during the summer months.

When the roots are running freely round the pots a liquid feed should be given weekly. A liquid feed made with sheep droppings was at one time very much favoured by professional gardeners.

In September the pots are returned to the house where they must be given ample ventilation and plenty of light. A temperature of 50 to 55°F. (10 to 13°C.) is ideal. Flowering will be had from late October until March or April.

Plants from corms are grown in much the same way as from seed. The corms are cleaned and repotted and started into growth during July and August and placed in a cold frame until taken into the house during September or early October.

As the plants grow and begin to flower ample room should be given so that a good circulation of air is maintained round the pots. Water with the greatest care during the winter. Never allow the compost to become quite dry and never over-water or this may easily bring about the collapse of the plant.

After flowering the plants should be rested by gradually with-holding water and during the summer the pots containing the old corms can be placed outside on their sides to dry off, before re-starting them into growth in the autumn.

There are various strains of this popular plant to be had as will be seen from any seedsmen's catalogue. The Marbled Leaved cycla-men has most attractive silvery zones on the leaves and flowers of normal size. There is also a strain with fringed petals.

Freesia. Few plants have attained greater popularity in recent years than freesias. The flowers are lovely in form and colour and their fragrance and long lasting quality when cut is hard to equal.

Freesias are not a difficult crop to grow and will be quite happy in a house where the minimum temperature does not fall below 45°F. (7°C.). Cool treatment and ample ventilation is in fact essen-tial for this crop and any attempt to force should be avoided.

Seed is sown during April or May in mild heat. The seed has a very hard coat and soaking in water heated to approximately 70°F. (21°C.) for twenty four hours before sowing is helpful. Many grow-ers chit the seed in damp peat and sand. In a temperature of 64°F. (18°C.) the seed will soon sprout, when it can be carefully sown. Direct sowings can be made in a temperature of approximately

64°F. but germination will be slower and rather irregular. Seed can also be sown in a deep pan or seed tray and the seedlings planted into 5 or 6 in. pots. The seedlings must be handled with extreme care as they resent being moved. When planting them take care not to damage the tender roots and see that the roots hang straight down. Nor must the seedlings be allowed to become too large. The optimum time to prick out seems to be when they are at the one and a half leaf stage, viz. the "whole" leaf being about 1½ in. tall and the second leaf about ¾ in. long.

Seven or eight seeds can be sown in a 6 in. pot filled with J.I.P.2 taking care to well crock the pot. Five plants will be enough for a 5 in. pot but sow two or three extra seeds in any case and after germination thin them to the number needed. Sow the seeds at a depth of ½ in. Water the pots via a fine rose and stand them in a warm position but once germination is complete move them to a cooler position.

In June the pots can be moved to the cold frame where they can remain until the autumn. Keep the lights on for a few days admitting air by propping up the light at the back. The light can then be removed and only replaced during heavy rain or strong wind. Place the pots on wood slats as the plant sends down long tender feeding roots that somehow get through the most unlikely cracks and penetrate into the ash base. If these are broken when the pots are moved a bad check is had.

During the summer see that the pots never dry out and keep them free from weed growth; little attention is needed other than keeping a close watch for aphides and thrips.

Towards the end of September the pots should be cleaned up and taken into the house. The fast growing foliage will need some support. This can be done by means of twiggy stakes or by inserting three or four canes round the pot and running fillis from cane to cane. An occasional liquid feed should be given.

No heat will be necessary for a short time but as the weather becomes colder a little heat will be needed if only to ensure air circulation. During the winter there should be no difficulty in growing good freesias if a minimum temperature of 45°F. (7°C.) is maintained. Flowering from seed should start towards the end of November.

After flowering ease off the watering and allow the foliage to die down. The pots can then be placed outside. A number of corms will be found to have formed and if these are well harvested the largest will give good flowers the next year.

Production from corms is much the same as from seed, except that corms are planted during August or September. The tips of the corms must be ¾ in. below the surface of the soil. After planting give a good watering and place the pots outside in a cool and shady place. The young grass-like shoots will appear in two or three weeks and the pots can then be stood in a frame if this has not already been done. Here the pots can remain until taken into the house, but early frosts must be guarded against by slipping over the lights if frost is forecast. The plants should be safely housed by the end of October and flowering should be had during February.

Where blooms are needed for cutting a convenient sized box 6 in. deep can be used and the seeds or corms placed at 2 in. square intervals.

It pays to buy good seed or corms. Amongst the finest strains are the K and M (Konynenburg and Mark) strain, Parigo strain and the Rainbow strain (Alois Frey, California).

Primula. The species of primula mostly grown in the greenhouse are *P. malacoides, P. sinensis* and *P. obconica. P. kewensis* is grown to a lesser extent and is particularly useful for a cold house. All the primulas are happy under cool conditions and should form part of any greenhouse collection.

P. Malacoides. This lovely little plant is one of the outstanding subjects for a cool house and embraces shades of rose-pink, lilac, mauve, white and red. The dainty little flowers are carried in whorls on stiff stems some 9 in. in length. Cultivation is easy for the plant is almost hardy. Sowings made during April and again in June will provide flowers from December until April.

Sow in a light and well moistened compost. Cover with glass and paper until germination is had. The seed is small and should be scattered over the surface of the compost and covered with the merest sprinkling of sand.

If water is needed the pan should be partly immersed in aired water.

When the seedlings can be handled they should be pricked off into 3 in. pots. Leave them in the house until they are established and then move them to a cool frame. Ample ventilation is needed and the plants never allowed to become dry.

P. malacoides is often flowered in 3 or 3½ in. pots but it is better, when the small pots become full of roots, to pot on into 5 in. pots, using the J.I.P.2. Do not set the plants too low in the compost and do not overfirm them. The plants should be brought into the house in mid-October for early flowering, but later batches can remain in the frame until November.

P. sinensis. This is a larger plant than *P. malacoides* and an old favourite. The seed is sown in April, June and July to ensure a continuity of flowering, but where time and space does not permit of too many plants a June sowing will provide a show quite early in the year and over a considerable period. Germination is somewhat irregular.

Pricking off and potting on follows the same procedure as with *P. malacoides* and it should again be mentioned that primulas should never be planted too deeply but should be left so that the lower leaves just clear the surface of the soil.

During August the more forward plants will be ready for their final potting into 5 in. pots. Very vigorous plants will benefit by being given a rather larger pot. The J.I.P.2 compost is very suitable. After the final potting the plants can be stood back in the frame until early October when they are taken into the greenhouse. Watering, feeding and ventilation must be strictly attended to. Never let the soil dry out but never over-water so that the compost becomes sodden and airless. The plants will need a stake. *P. stellata* is treated in exactly the same way but will make a taller plant and will not object to rather more warmth.

P. obconica. This is the primula that can cause a form of dermatitis. It does not affect the majority of people but if one is allergic to any skin trouble it is well to leave this plant along.

P. obconica is an extremely showy plant and a section of staging filled with these plants in full bloom can be a blaze of colour. The range of colours include rose, salmon, crimson, blue, lavender and lilac. A packet of mixed Gigantia will provide all these colours, or if preferred seed can be obtained in separate colours.

The seed is even more irregular in germination than *P. sinensis* and as soon as the first seedlings appear any paper covering should be removed from the pan and the glass raised at one end to admit air. Culture is the same as for other species and a sowing made in May or June will provide a wealth of colour in the early spring and flowering will extend over a considerable period. Summer treatment, housing and attention to ventilation and shading is again similar to other greenhouse primulas. Shading from bright sun during the early spring is necessary or the plants will quickly wilt.

Polyanthus. The modern strains of these delightful and well known plants are very suitable for pot culture, for they bring colour into the house in the very early days of spring.

Strains of the Pacific Hybrids should be potted up in a loamy, compost in the early autumn. Well developed plants that have been pricked out from an early spring sowing should be potted up into 5 in. pots. Keep them in the frame under cool conditions until December when they should be brought into the house in succession to provide flowering plants over a lengthy period from the early spring onwards. They should be given the same cool treatment as other primulas.

13

Tomatoes and Cucumbers

From the utility angle tomatoes and cucumbers are two of the most popular crops for the greenhouse. Ideally both should be grown in separate houses but few amateurs will feel they can devote a house entirely to either. In so many cases the house will be given over to flowering plants during the winter and spring plus a number of tomato plants during the summer. It is possible, where the house is large enough, to divide off a small section at the end by means of polythene sheeting hung from roof to floor and grow cucumbers in this section. The chief reason for this is that while the tomatoes need a buoyant atmosphere the cucumbers must have just the opposite—a steamy and almost turkish bath-like condition.

TOMATOES

Tomatoes are often grown on one side of the house and a mixed bag of other subjects that will not object to partial shade on the less sunny side. Where possible tomatoes are better grown in the border, but excellent crops are had when they are grown in pots or boxes on the staging. In a small house with high side walls the staging is a better place, as the borders will be dark.

Once the seedlings are raised and planted out no great heat is needed and during the warmer months artificial heat can be dispensed with. But a temperature of 55 to 60°F. (13 to 16°C.) is needed early in the season, and where heating is inadequate or there is no heating at all it is better to buy the plants from a nurseryman in early or mid-April and plant out during April or, in more exposed districts, in early May.

Where sufficient heat is available an early start can be made with a view to early cropping. Many professional growers sow as early as November, but January or February sowings are far less trouble for by then light intensity is increasing. Timing with regard to sowing is important and the date of sowing must be related to the probable date of planting out. Plants sown too soon and starved in small pots will not provide a profitable crop and if the staging or border is not ready the plants should be moved on into larger pots. Under average conditions the seed should be sown some six to seven weeks before planting out is anticipated.

So much has been written on tomato growing that it seems unnecessary here to detail cultivation from A to Z; nor does space permit. The principles of plant raising will be found in Chapter 9 but a word should be said with regard to soil preparation and general cultivation. The soil in the border should be double dug as early as possible and the need for organic replacement attended to. One good barrow-load of manure or good compost to each 10 square yards will be a good dressing. The need for moisture must not be overlooked and a good flooding should be given to replenish the underlying reserves. Lime is often needed in a greenhouse border and a 4 oz. per square yard dressing should be given after the initial digging, scattering it over the surface. Just before planting is to be done work into the top few inches a dressing of some complete fertiliser with a high potash content. A 5 oz. per square yard dressing of fish manure is recommended.

Sowings can be made in pans or seed trays and the seeds spaced at $1\frac{1}{2}$ in. apart in a light compost such as the J.I. Seed Compost. A temperature of 70°F. (21°C.) is not too high, but as soon as the seeds germinate—which should be in six or seven days—the temperature should be reduced to 60°F. (15°C.). Prick off singly into 3 in. pots as soon as the seedlings can be handled using the J.I.P.1. Give a watering via a fine rose and stand on the staging but provide shade from bright sunshine for a few days.

The actual time of planting out must depend on when the space becomes available and the temperature that can be maintained. From mid-March to mid-April will be the most popular time for planting out but it is most important if the plants are to get away unchecked that the soil should have warmed up. Where the house has been heated throughout the winter the soil temperature will be about right, but care must be taken to see that compost used for potting is warm and it should be brought into the house some time before potting is due. In passing it will be of interest to note that the temperature of the top few inches should ideally be in the region of 56 to 60°F. (13 to 15°C.).

Large pots or boxes placed on the staging will prove a better method of growing where, in a small house with deep side walls, the border may be badly lighted. The type of plant needed is a sturdy, short-jointed plant about 9 to 10 in. high and of a dark green colour. Avoid leggy plants or any that show abnormalities of any kind. Planting methods and distance will depend on the size of the border and the number of plants to be grown. With only a few plants allow 18 in. from plant to plant.

The J.I.P.3 or a similar mixture is very suitable for pots or boxes and when filling leave enough room for a dressing of soil later on. Spray the young plants with water twice a day for the first few days rather than over-watering at the roots.

As the plants grow permanent support must be given by means of stakes or fillis. When tying take care to leave room for the stem to thicken and remove any side shoots as they appear. Give the plants a syringing over with clear water on bright mornings. This will help to create a suitable atmosphere for pollination and during hot weather it may be advisable to damp down a second time during the afternoon. Avoid spraying or damping down on dull days but give a gentle shake to assist pollination. Water will be needed in more generous quantities as the plants grow and trusses form and some light shading should be given to break up the direct rays of the sun and to help in keeping the temperature steady.

Ventilation must always be generous and during summer nights the roof ventilators should be left open whenever possible. It is often said with regard to ventilation that whenever in doubt leave the ventilators open.

A top dressing of soil should be given in the case of pot plants and this should be done after the second or third truss has set. At this stage the plants often seem to hang fire and become less vigorous and a weekly liquid feed will be needed. Plants in pots or boxes will usually need rather earlier feeding than those in the border. Excellent proprietary liquid feeds can be had in concentrated form and these can be used with confidence.

Ring Culture. Considerable interest has been shown in this method of tomato growing. The plants are grown in bottomless pots or "rings" filled with a good compost and stood on a base of ashes, broken clinker, shingle, etc. A two zone system of roots is formed, the more fibrous roots being confined to the pots while the coarser water-seeking roots penetrate into the base (Fig. 43).

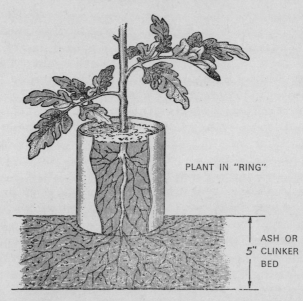

PLANT IN "RING"

ASH OR
5" CLINKER
BED

Fig. 43. Ring culture of tomatoes. A two-zone system of roots is built up

The advantage of this method is that tomatoes can be grown in a house where the border soil is physically unfit or contaminated with pests or disease. The fresh compost in the rings and the aggregate in the base provide a healthy and well drained growing medium.

The plants are set out in the rings in the usual way and for the first two or three weeks given normal treatment until roots start to penetrate into the base. At this point water is given only via the base and this can be done freely and without fear of over-watering, as any surplus water will quickly drain away. A liquid feed is given weekly or bi-weekly via the compost in the rings and never via the base.

A trench 5 in. deep is taken out along the border and filled with a suitable aggregate. If more convenient the aggregate can be contained within 6 in. boards. Where the border soil is known to be infected a sheet of polythene can be used to prevent the aggregate coming into contact with the soil. In this case drainage slits should be made in the polythene. The rings are stood on the base and filled with compost. The J.I.P.2 does very well and as only a 9 or 10 in. ring is necessary the compost will quickly warm up. Do not over-water the small plants during the first week or two but give about the same amount as they would require if they were still in 3 in. pots. Provided the aggregate is kept well watered this will ensure early root penetration into the base.

Straw Bales. Another method of recent introduction has been used with success by both commercial and amateur growers. Again, the method enables crops to be had where sterilising or the replacement of soil would be out of the question.

The bales of straw, usually of 56 lb. and with the wire ties retained are taken into the house and laid lengthwise along the border. Water is applied at intervals for three days and an average size bale of 56 lb. should have absorbed some nine gallons of water by the end of the period. Fermentation is brought about by spreading nitro-chalk (21 per cent N.) on top of each bale. An initial dressing of $1\frac{1}{2}$ lb. should be given and further dressings of 1 lb. and one of $\frac{1}{4}$ lb. are given over the next few days. Each dressing must be watered in. With the last dressing of nitro-chalk add 18 oz. of potassium nitrate, 10 oz. of triple superphosphate and 4 oz. of magnesium sulphate per bale.

Fermentation will soon take place and with further watering the temperature inside the bales should reach about 120°F. in five or six days in a house with a temperature of 50°F. On top of the bales a small mound of equal parts loam and peat or J.I.P.2 are made at the required intervals along the bales and the plants set in these.

The roots will soon penetrate into the bales where they find an ideally warm and healthy root-run. Nutrients by way of a weekly liquid feed should be given after the first truss has set.

CUCUMBERS

It is difficult to grow cucumbers in a mixed house for reasons already stated and a separate section of the house is really necessary or better still a low narrow type of house, for a low house will hold atmospheric moisture more easily and be more economic to heat. Where it is impossible to curtain off a section some sort of compromise can be made if one must attempt to grow cucumbers with tomatoes and other subjects. The cucumbers should be grown at the further end of the house and a variety chosen that will stand up to a drier atmosphere. The variety Conqueror is the best and L.M.R.1 or Vetomould are tomato varieties that are practically immune from leaf-mould.

Cucumbers are grown on a bed or ridge either on the staging or on the floor of the house. A compost composed of two parts turfy loam and one of old strawy manure plus enough sharp sand to keep the mixture open is used. To this should be added a liberal sprinkling of bonemeal and a little lime. Roughly a bushel of compost should be allowed for each plant. When the bed is made in the form of a low ridge it should be approximately 20 in. at the base, 12 in. wide at the top and 10 in. high.

The time to sow the seed will depend on when planting is to be undertaken and the temperature that can be given. In the spring six weeks must be allowed before planting is due. A start can be made very early in the year but such an early crop is difficult and expensive and a March or April sowing will be far easier and allow the house to be used for a previous crop.

Sowing is better done direct in 3 in. pots lightly filled with an open compost. Half loam and half peat with sharp sand will do nicely. Push each seed in edgeways to a depth of $\frac{3}{4}$ in. but do not firm the compost. Moisten with aired water, place the pots where they will get the benefit of bottom heat and cover with glass or, better still, place them in a propagator. A temperature of 70°F. (21°C.) is desirable. Under these conditions germination will be had in a few days. Syringe over the seedlings daily but keep them shaded. Move into larger pots where the roots are freely running round the pots using the J.I.P.2 or a similar mixture. Syringe over daily keeping the roots nicely moist but never too wet. Support the plants with a short cane as the stem lengthens.

Planting out should not be done until the prepared bed has warmed through. Give the plants a ball watering before knocking them out of the pots and plant on top of the ridge or mound. Planting is best done by pulling back sufficient soil with the hands to take the plant and then lightly pressing the soil back round the roots. The top of the ball should be slightly higher than the level of the bed. Give shade if the weather is sunny. Cucumbers must be grown quickly and a temperature of 60 to 65°F. (15 to 19°C.) should be aimed at.

The plants are trained on horizontal wires fixed 6 or 8 in. apart by means of "vine eyes". These eyes allow the wires to stand out well away from the glass. The main shoot is first tied to a short cane until it reaches the first horizontal wire and tied in turn to each wire until it reaches the apex of the roof when it is stopped. Meanwhile laterals will have formed and as these lengthen they

Installing space heating cables in a frame. Note how cables follow the slope of the frame. The transformer is for soil warming wires.

Soil warming. Connecting the galvanised iron wires to the low voltage side of the transformer. A mains voltage cable with insulating and protective sheathings can be connected direct to the mains supply.

The I.C.I. polythene cloche tunnel. The tunnel is easy to erect, the polythene being supported on strong metal hoops and securing wires.

A well grown crop of lettuce under Barn cloches. Sown mid-October and ready to cut in early April.

A promising crop of early strawberries. The variety is Royal Sovereign.

Syringing over dwarf beans growing under cloches. A good variety for early sowing under cloches or frames is "The Prince".

Cucumbers grown under cloches. The variety is Conqueror.

Asters as pot plants. The new Milady (Rose and Blue) bears a profusion of large incurved blooms on dwarf plants and might almost be taken for dwarf chrysanthemums.

are trained along the horizontal wires and stopped when they are some 12 in. long. Sub-laterals will quickly appear and these too must be tied to the wires. Each fruiting lateral should be pinched back two leaves beyond the fruits. Unlike melons cucumbers do not need pollinating and male flowers and tendrils should be picked off (Fig. 44).

It is important to keep the plants shaded from bright sun and a semi-permanent shading such as Summer Cloud should be

Fig. 44. Cucumbers on the staging. A cane should be used to support the plant until it reaches the horizontal wires

applied. A warm and moist bed is essential and it must never be allowed to dry out but at the same time it must not be overwatered or it will become cold and airless and root trouble will surely follow. A humid atmosphere is maintained by syringing over the plants twice a day with aired water and damping down the bed and paths. On dull days less damping down will be needed. Ventilation is necessary at times to give a change of air and to help keep the temperature within limits.

As soon as any roots appear on the surface of the bed a mulch of soil should be given and a feed of dried blood (2 oz. per gallon of water) given during the cropping season. Cucumbers crop in flushes and the first feed should be given after the first flush and between successive flushes.

When watering take care not to water immediately round the base of the stem. Stagnant water will bring about canker at this point and cause the plant to collapse. More harm is done to cucumbers by over-watering than by giving too little, and the aim should be to maintain a nicely moist bed that is warm and comfortable to the touch.

Straw bales are often used for cucumbers as well as for tomatoes and where loam is difficult to obtain or soil conditions unsuitable this method can be well recommended.

Good varieties of cucumbers for the amateur are Improved Telegraph and Butchers Disease Resisting. A new FI hybrid introduced by Messrs. Suttons called "Femspot" produces only female flowers.

14

Some Popular Plants for the Stove-House

The stove or hot-house is a house for the connoisseur and calls for a high degree of skill and understanding for the plants to be grown will not, unlike many other subjects, easily adapt themselves to conditions other than those near to what they would find in their natural habitat. To maintain a collection of tropical plants at least some artificial heat will be needed throughout the year except, perhaps, on hot summer nights. A minimum night temperature of about 60°F. (18°C.) from October to April will be needed and roughly 70°F. (21°C.) during the rest of the year.

It is seldom today that the average amateur grower can devote one entire house to tropical plants but as mentioned earlier in this book a portion of a temperate house can be partitioned off and if additional warmth is provided by means of extra pipes, used successfully as a hot house.

The management of a stove-house will call for much more than stoking up the boiler to give a high temperature, for a constantly moist atmosphere must be maintained and this will call for more than the ordinary damping down associated with other types of houses. The staging should be of galvanised iron sheeting, cement-asbestos sheets or slate and covered with 2 in. of fine shingle or some similar moisture retaining material. The pathway should preferably be of bricks rather than concrete and the remainder of the floor area covered with ashes or small breeze. All this will ensure ample moisture retention to be gradually released by the warmth from the pipes. The methodical and regular damping down over all parts of the house, staging and floor as well as the plants will be necessary. During the summer this will usually be necessary twice a day but in winter a daily syringing between plants on the staging and damping over the floor will keep the atmosphere moist while syringing over the plants at this time is kept down to a minimum. A tank inside the house should be provided for water storage so that syringing over and watering can be carried out with water at the same temperature as the house.

During winter these warm and humid conditions must be accompanied by unrestricted light and the glass must therefore be kept free from dirt. In summer shade must be given and blinds that can be rolled up or down as needed should be used rather than any form of permanent or semi-permanent shading. Full light can then be given during the earlier part of the morning and in the late afternoon. On dull days no shading will be necessary.

Ventilation must be provided for as in any other type of house, but it must be so arranged that draughts are avoided. In this connection an electric extraction fan thermostatically controlled will automatically bring about air changes and heat control. Because of the high humidity in a stove house any electrical installation must be well sealed against moisture.

It is of interest to remember that stove or tropical houses built at the beginning of the century were of teak. The cost was higher but the extra outlay was repaid over and over again because teak was so very durable. Glass was normally cut with a curved lower edge. This tended to cause rainwater to gather in the middle of the panes, thus assisting in preserving woodwork and putty. A further refinement adopted for the stove-house was to build in double doors. On passing through the outer door one entered a small glassed in lobby with a further door which had to be opened before entering the main greenhouse. Doors were spring loaded and thus the two in theory were never open at the same time. This prevented draughts and the dropping of the temperature when the gardener entered or left the greenhouse. This gives an idea of the lengths to which the keen grower would go in his efforts to obtain optimum conditions.

The following list of plants are those which are amongst the better known and more popular plants for the hot house and within the skill of the average amateur grower. It is by no means complete and the interested grower will find others listed in Chapter 17. A visit to the glasshouses connected with the Parks Department of your nearest town will probably reveal many other fascinating subjects for a hot-house, especially foliage plants used for decorative purposes.

There is no doubt that a stove-house can be an expensive hobby and demanding in time and skill but the results can be most rewarding and well worth time and effort.

Acalypha. Evergreen shrubs grown largely for their foliage. One of the most popular is *A. hispida*, sometimes called Red Hot Cats-tail. Other varieties have leaves of orange, red, green and crimson. A compost of peat, leafmould and sand in equal parts seems to suit the plants and like all plants in the stove-house ample drainage must be provided. Potting and pruning should be done in spring. Propagation is by cuttings struck in a sandy soil in early spring.

Adiantum. These lovely ferns can be grown in the warmer conditions of the stove-house and will even produce young plants by sporing naturally in all sorts of corners. *A. bausei* and *A. tenerum farleyense* are suitable for the stove-house (see also page 175).

Aechmea. This is the Greek Vase Plant and reasonably easy to grow. It is an evergreen stove flowering plant. A compost of fibrous loam, peat and a little sharp sand will suit it. Propagation is by the removal of offsets which root quite easily. Water that may lie in the bottom of the "vase" will do no harm.

Agapetes. A. macrantha is a very beautiful evergreen greenhouse climber which should be trained under the greenhouse roof so that the clusters of tube-like flowers can hang and be seen to advantage. In a house with a minimum temperature of 55°F. (13°C.) it makes a splendid show during the winter. The flowers are 1½ to 2 in. long and white with reddish markings.

It should be grown in a lime free compost and moist and warm conditions are needed.

It is propagated by cuttings taken in the spring from shoots of the previous year and inserted in peat and sand in a propagating frame. A temperature of 65 to 70°F. (18 to 21°C.) is needed.

Ananas. The Pineapple. See page 173.

Anthurium. This is often called the Flamingo Flower from the bright scarlet spathes which last for several months. This fascinating plant hails from tropical America and belongs to the arum family.

Potting is done in the early spring as soon as new roots begin to develop. The pots must be nearly half filled with crocks. A suitable compost will be three parts peat, one part sphaghum moss, a little loam and some charcoal. A sprinkling of silver sand should be added to this mixture. The roots must be kept high in the pot by planting on a slight mound and packing more compost round the roots. A pot of 6 or 7 in. will be needed for a plant of any size.

Propagate in February by dividing the rootstock. The favourite kind for greenhouse work is *A. scherzerianum. A. andreanum* has larger spathes and leaves. *A. crystallium* is a species with most attractive velvety-green leaves with prominent white veins.

Aphelandra. The Zebra plant. A very popular house plant available from most florists. The leaves of varying shades of green have most attractive white veins. The flower at the top of the stem is surrounded by a cone of yellow bracts and these too are attractive in the summer and autumn. Like many stove plants a peaty soil is required and good drainage is essential. Old plants after flowering can be pruned by cutting hard back.

Propagate by taking side shoots with a heel in spring inserted in pots of sharp sand and placed in a warm propagating frame. *A. squarrosa* and its variety Louisae is the usual variety grown.

Aristolochia. These are climbers which require plenty of room and produce elegant foliage and large and interesting flowers of unusual shape during the summer. It is also known as the Dutchman's Pipe. Loam plus a little peat and sand will suit the plant and pruning consists of superfluous shoots to prevent overcrowding. Wires must be fixed to the roof as supports for the twining stems.

Propagation is by cuttings taken during spring and summer.

Brunfelsia. Evergreen flowering shrubs with lovely flowers produced over a long period. It is sometimes called Franciscea. A strong loam with added peat and sand will form a suitable compost. After flowering, the shoots are shortened by half and frequent syringing carried out to encourage fresh growth.

Propagation is by cuttings taken in spring and summer. It is seen to advantage when allowed to climb along wires fixed under the roof of the house.

Caladium. This is a plant grown for its arrow headed foliage and they come in great variety and size. It is a tuberous rooted plant and during the summer when growth is rapid it requires a mixture of a light loam, peat, sand and a little charcoal. In autumn as the plant dies down water is withheld and the tubers are stored for the winter in warm dry soil or left in the pots in which they grew. The tubers are restarted into growth and repotted the following spring. Propagation is by natural division of tubers.

Calathea. See Maranta.

Clerodendron. Clerodendron fragrans is another climbing plant and suitable for the stove-house. *C. fallax* is a non-climbing species and a great favourite. The foliage is rather large and the plants bear panicles of orange-scarlet flowers in summer.

Equal parts of loam, peat and leafmould plus sharp sand make an excellent compost; the loam should not be broken down too finely but left on the lumpy side. Pot in early spring and grow in a temperature of 65 to 75°F. (18 to 21°C.). Liberal supplies of water are needed during the summer.

C. fallax is easily raised from seed sown in a light compost during March. Place the pan in a propagator with a temperature of 70°F. (21°C.).

Codiæum (Croton). These are grown for their leaves which are variegated with brilliant colours ranging from yellow to orange-pink, red and crimson. It is best to raise plants annually as the colours are more vivid on the young plants.

Cuttings are rooted in spring and summer in sandy soil and plunged in fibre in a closed and warm propagating case until rooted. They are then potted off separately in small pots and returned to the propagating case until they are established. They are then stood on the staging and later potted on into 5 in. pots.

A good compost consists of equal parts of fibrous loam and peat with some sharp sand added. A moist atmosphere must be maintained.

Columnea. A not too difficult plant belonging to the Gesneria family. Some species are very suitable for baskets. The flowers are generally orange and red in colour. They like a peaty compost and propagation is by cuttings. See also page 188.

Cordyline. The Cordylines and Dracænas are fairly similar and they are plants liking very warm moist conditions and are grown for the wonderful range of foliage. They require a little shade and should be given a rich compost with some old manure added.

Propagation is by cutting up old stems and rooting them or by side cuttings and even by rooting underground shoots.

Croton. See Codiæum.

Davallia. The Hare's Foot Fern. A dainty fern to grow in the stove-house.

Dieffenbachia. Dumb Cane or Mother-in-Law Plant. Another group of plants grown for their foliage. The plants should not come into contact with the mouth as its effect may be most unpleasant. The compost should be fairly strong. It can be propagated from suckers or by pieces of the stem cut up with an eye and rooted.

Gardenia. A shrub with scented white flowers. Makes an ideal buttonhole. It requires a rich soil with plenty of moisture but avoid wetting the blooms when they are out. It can be rooted from cuttings.

Gesneria. An attractive flowering plant for the stove house. The foliage is an added attraction. Like the Columnia it requires a peaty soil and it can be propagated by its tubers or cuttings of young growth and even seed. It is also possible to propagate it from leaves pegged down on peat or inserted stalk end in sandy compost. After flowering the plant should be dried off and rested in a warm house. The Naegelias can be given similar treatment.

Maranta. Hot house ornamental leaved plants. The leaves vary in shape and size and are beautifully marked with blotches and streaks of contrasting colours.

Equal parts of loam and peat and half part of sharp sand forms a very suitable compost. The pots must be well drained for the plant will need ample water supplies during the summer, but much less in winter. When potting the compost should not be pressed down unduly.

The principal method of propagation is by way of division in February when the roots should be washed clean and the rhizomes cut through with a sharp knife. The cut surface should be dipped in charcoal to prevent rotting.

Monstera. The species usually grown is *M. deliciosa.* It has immense dark green leaves perforated with holes and bears yellow flowers and fruits with a flavour somewhat resembling pineapple and banana. The plants can be grown in large pots or tubs but they are better, where room permits, planted in a border when they make large climbing plants and produce the edible fruits.

A rich loamy soil is required and during the spring and summer ample water supplies are needed and the leaves syringed over. Much less water is needed during the winter. Any repotting that becomes necessary should be done in February or March.

Propagation is by means of cuttings taken in the spring or summer. They will need placing in a propagating frame with bottom heat.

Nepenthes. The Pitcher Plant. These catch insects in the curious formation at the end of the leaves. Grow them in baskets and hang them from the roof of the greenhouse. The compost should be mainly loam fibre and sphagnum moss. They require a little shade and must have plenty of water and warmth. Propagation is by seed sown on peat and sphagnum in a high temperature or by cuttings of shoots plunged over bottom heat.

Nephrolepis. Another hot house fern with dense finely cut fronds. Commonly known as the Ladder Fern. It requires a peaty soil and can be planted in baskets, in pots or in a bed. Like most ferns water should be given moderately in winter but freely in summer. It can be propagated by spores, by division of plants in spring or by rooting the creeping stems.

Peperomia. Another large group of plants grown for their ornamental foliage. It is commonly called Pepper Elder. The compost should be of fibrous loam and peat with a little sand. Propagation is by cuttings of shoots or by leaves with a little shoot attached.

Persea. This is the Avocado or Alligator Pear. It is a stove evergreen shrub with edible purplish fruit. The compost should be of loam, peat and some sand and much water is required in summer but little in winter. It will make a large shrub given the right conditions. Propagation is by seeds or by cuttings rooted in a propagating case in spring (see Chapter 16 page 172).

Platycerium. The Stag's Head Fern. This fern should be grown on blocks of wood or slabs of thick cork and under suitable conditions will make fronds of two feet or more in length. The fronds fork very freely and hence the name.

Stephanotis. A climbing evergreen plant for the hot-house. The leaves are fleshy and of a deep shining green. It produces large clusters of delightfully scented flowers during the summer months. The flowers are white and tubular in shape extending to five petals at the tips. The flowers are in great demand by the florists. The species commonly grown is *S. floribunda*.

It is best to grow this plant in a prepared bed of good soil but they can also be grown in large pots so long as a regular feed is given during the spring and summer. In the early spring some of the old top soil should be removed and the plant top dressed with fresh compost. Train the shoots along horizontal wires beneath the roof.

Propagation is by cuttings taken in the spring of the previous year's growth. These cuttings will root freely if placed in a warm and closed propagating frame.

Strelitzia. There are several species of this genus, the one largely grown is *S. regina* and aptly called the Bird of Paradise Flower. It is a large plant that is best planted in the border but will succeed in tubs in the stove house. It has large handsome leaves on long strong leafstalks and bears brilliant flowers of blue and yellow looking somewhat like a bird in flight. It requires a very rich compost and during the growing season copious supplies of water and a humid atmosphere.

It is increased by removing side shoots or by digging up and dividing the plant in spring. It will succeed in a temperate house if the minimum temperature is not less than 55°F. (13°C.).

This list should be viewed as suggestions as in most cases we have not gone deeply into the variations within the species. Some of the plants can be grown in somewhat lower temperatures than the stove-house provides but they cannot be expected to succeed as well as they would in a higher temperature. Cleanliness in the stove-house is of vital importance because once any infestation gets established the conditions are such that it will spread quickly. Most stove plants follow the pattern of plenty of moisture in the summer, far less in winter when growth is much limited. Composts suggested do not include fertilisers and it is assumed that you will have a good source of fibrous loam which in most cases will form the basis of the compost. Many of them will succeed in soil-less composts and in most cases the ideal method of feeding is to apply liquid feeds during the active growing season.

15

Vegetables in the Greenhouse

The production of vegetables in a general purpose house is somewhat limited. While it is true that commercial growers succeed in producing at an early date a range of vegetable crops normally grown outdoors the amateur will not be sufficiently interested to think of erecting the more spacious structures that such crops need. Nor will many vegetables fit in well with the general programme carried out in the small house. The amateur gardener would do better to use a Dutch light house or some similar structure with glass almost to the ground and grow direct in the soil of the house. Crops are produced successfully in the light and airy conditions such houses provide and with a little heat food crops can be had practically throughout the year. But in pots or boxes on the staging of a small house few of these crops can be successfully grown even if room can be found for them.

Few of our vegetables are happy under the warm and closer conditions of the average general purpose house, but certain crops will succeed in company with other subjects especially where a border can be used on one side of the house. There are also forcing crops needing the higher temperatures that can be given and which often can be accommodated under the staging. Nor should the usefulness of a moderately heated house be forgotten for raising such subjects as cauliflowers, celery, onion, lettuce, marrows, peas and beans for planting outside as soon as weather permits.

Dwarf French Beans. This is a crop grown very successfully in the greenhouse and will provide very early pickings. Space can often be found for a few pots on the staging or shelves and sowings can also be made in a border.

Sowings are often made as early as October, but a January or February sowing is more usual and less exacting. Dwarf beans like a fairly high temperature but providing a steady day temperature of about 55°F. (13°C.) and not less than 40 to 45°F. (5 to 7°C.) at night tender young beans will be had in May.

Four plants can be grown in an 8 in. pot or three in a 7 in. pot, using the J.I.P.2 or a similar mixture. Half fill the pot with the compost and sow six or seven seeds in each 1 in. deep and thin the resulting seedlings to the required number. The seeds will germinate better, and are less likely to rot or damp off, if the compost is kept rather on the dry side. Once the seeds are sown do not water again until they are growing away. When a good root system has formed watering should be a little more generous.

As the plants grow more soil must be added until the pots are filled to within an inch of the top, and watering can then be even a little more generous. A weekly feed of manure water should be given as soon as the flowers begin to set and a syringing over with aired water should be given daily during fine weather. This will not only help the plants but discourage red spider and thrips.

Some support by way of twiggy sticks should be given or short canes placed round the pots and fillis run from cane to cane to hold the plants up as they become heavy with pods. Good varieties are The Prince, the earliest, and Masterpiece, a tremendous cropper and a good variety for the border.

The French Climbing bean is also grown for early work in the greenhouse. It is treated in the same way as the Dwarf Bean but will, of course, need the support of large pea boughs or fillis. It can be grown in pots and trained up fillis at the back of a lean-to house. The variety needed is Tender and True. Do not attempt to grow the ordinary runner in the greenhouse.

Lettuce. Pot or box culture is sometimes recommended for lettuce, but it is a somewhat chancy method and a deep box or a 5 in. pot is needed. Where a border can be used a good crop can be had with far less trouble and lettuces cut from November until the early spring when frame or cloche lettuce will be available. No great heat is needed but a minimum night temperature of 40 to 45°F. (5 to 7°C.) should be maintained. The secret of a constant supply lies in making small sowings at intervals from September until January. Many varieties specially bred for the dark days can be had and include Chestnut Early Giant, 5B, Amplus, Winterpride, Delta Kordaat, etc. Sowings of Amplus made in early September can be ready in late November and December, while a late September/

October sowing of Amplus or Winterpride will be ready from December to February. These all need mild heat. Sowings made in a cold house of Delta or Attractie will be ready to cut in late March or early April.

The soil of the border must be fertile and contain plenty of humus material. The surface of the soil must be worked to a fine tilth and the seed sown *in situ* and thinned out later to stand at 9 in. each way. Seed can also be sown in seed-trays and pricked out. The practice of sowing pelleted seed *in situ* can be an advantage for these lettuce sowings.

The bed should be well watered before sowing and great care taken never to allow the soil to become dry. When watering, water between the plants rather than over them. Watch out for aphis and deal with them as soon as seen. Spraying with a systemic insecticide as a precautionary measure is better than waiting until the pests have established themselves.

Always give sufficient ventilation to keep the temperature steady. This is particularly important in February and March when a burst of sun can send the temperature soaring to a dangerous level resulting in leaf scorch.

Aubergines. Aubergines or Egg Plants provide a summer dish very much favoured on the Continent where the purple fruits are great favourites. In these days of travel many will have enjoyed this excellent vegetable and would like to grow it.

The plant is an annual and should be sown during February or in early March in a temperature of 65°F. (18°C.). A propagating frame with bottom heat does very nicely or the seed pan can be placed above the hot pipes and covered with glass. As soon as the seedlings have made two leaves they should be pricked off separately into 3 in. pots using the J.I.P.1 or a soil-less mix. In quite a short time the plants will need moving into larger pots and eventually into fruiting pots of 7 or 8 in. It is important in the early stages to keep the plants moving and at no time must they be allowed to become pot-bound. For the final potting the J.I.P.3 can be used.

Aubergines like a warm and sunny position and plenty of moisture when established. They also like a syringing over twice daily during hot weather and this should not be neglected especially as red spider can be a serious pest on these plants.

When the plant is 6 in. high the growing point should be pinched out to induce a branching habit and the side shoots stopped a leaf or two beyond the fruit. Once the flowers start to set a weekly feed of liquid manure should be given. Four to six fruits per plant are ample for pot plants.

There are a number of varieties but the favourite is Long Purple.

Capsicum. Capsicum or Pepper is another vegetable the traveller will have met with abroad and, like the aubergine, is fast becoming better known in this country. It can be had at an early date when grown in the greenhouse and if the pods are left to colour they form most attractive plants—particularly the small podded chilli.

For greenhouse work sow in early March and grow on in 6 in. pots using a rich compost. They should be stood in a sunny place in the house and need a moderate temperature. The oddly shaped and wrinkled pods are picked as soon as they are large enough and while still green (see also page 46).

Carrots. Carrots can be had very early if grown in the greenhouse. A border, of course, is the best place for them but they can be grown in boxes on the staging if room can be found for them. A box 4 or 5 in. deep is needed.

The best type to grow is one of the early forcing varieties of short-horn or Early Gem. The latter is a good variety for the border where they can be grown between lettuce as an inter-crop. The seeds can also be broadcast, taking care to sow very sparsely. Late January or early February is the time to sow.

Turnips. Early turnips are very welcome and can be sown in early February. Early White Milan or Suttons Early Snowball should be sown in the border and thinned to stand at 3 to 4 in. apart. Both carrots and turnips need to be grown quickly and they will need generous watering. Do not give any fresh manure when preparing the bed. Both can be grown in a cold house but they will not be ready quite so soon, and sowing may have to be deferred until February if the weather is unsuitable.

Radish. Small sowings of radishes from time to time can be made either as a catch crop between other crops in the border or in boxes or large pots. A few radishes are often welcome during the dark months to add to a salad. A pinch of seed sown at almost any time during the winter, but particularly from January onwards, will supply the small quantity generally needed. French Breakfast or Scarlet Globe are good varieties for these sowings.

Beetroot. Here again succulent young roots can be had from the border of a greenhouse. Like turnips, beetroots must be grown quickly and a start can be made early in February in mild heat. A cold house will serve, but a house with moderate heat will produce earlier roots. Details of cultivation will be found on page 45. Suttons Early Bunch or Scarlet Globe are varieties suitable for early work in the greenhouse.

Mustard and Cress. Both are so easy to grow that little need be said as to cultivation. A constant supply can be had by making successive sowings in quite shallow boxes. See that the soil is nicely moist before sowing. If the box is covered with another of similar size inverted over the first the stems will quickly become long. At this point the box of M. and C. should be given full light to give colour to the stems and leaves. Do not cover the seed but press it on to the damp compost and cut with a pair of scissors or a very sharp knife. Always remember to sow the cress four days before the mustard if you want to use them together. Early supplies will need some heat but the produce will be most valuable in the kitchen.

Forcing Rhubarb. An essential condition for forcing rhubarb is complete darkness and a space under the staging can easily be prepared by covering a slatted staging with an asbestos-cement sheet and closing the sides with wood, canvas or more asbestos sheeting. Thick sacks will be convenient to cover in the front. A piece of wood or asbestos should be placed in front of the pipes to prevent undue drying out of the soil.

Three- or four-year-old crowns are the best for forcing. Fortunately only two or three roots will be needed where the demand is modest but where a continuity of supply is looked for the supply of roots becomes a problem in a small garden. Where room is available a few new sets should be planted each spring to grow on.

Place a 3 or 4 in. layer of good soil on the floor and on this stand the old roots closely together. Pack the spaces between the roots with fine soil pushed well down with the fingers until only the tips of the crowns are seen. Now give a good watering with tepid water

Cineraria multiflora. An indispensible subject for the cool house. Successive sowings will ensure a display from December until April or May.

An early crop of carrots growing under cloches.

A well grown head of Heliotrope (Cherry Pie) A fragrant and beautiful subject for the greenhouse. The variety is "Marine".

Freesia seedling in a 7 in. pot from an April sowing. Corms can be planted during August.

Cyclamen (Suttons Triumph). Superb plants for the greenhouse blooming from the late autumn onwards until late spring.

Primula malacoides (the Fairy Primula) A dainty and popular plant for the late autumn and winter. A cold frame during the summer and a cool house in the winter is needed.

via a fine rose. The roots must now be completely darkened and only exposed for the briefest periods for attention. Give a light spraying over each day and watch out for any woodlice. Water as necessary.

A temperature of 45°F. (7°C.) is best to start with but this can be increased later on to 50° or even 60°F. (10 to 15°C.). Rhubarb can still be forced at 40°F. (5°C.). Although naturally it will be slower.

The old roots should be lifted during October and left in the open to weather, when they will force more readily. The sticks should be pulled when they are some 15 or 16 in. long. Varieties for forcing—Royal Albert, The Sutton and Dawes Champion.

Asparagus. Asparagus may be forced by lifting a few roots of three or four years old plants and placing them on a bed of soil in a deep box. A bed of old potting soil about 3 in. deep can also be made in a warm corner of the house. Lay the roots on the soil and cover with 2 or 3 in. of fine soil. Give a good watering and see that the roots never get dry.

When growth is seen give enough light to green the shoots and cut when they are 6 or 7 in. long. Once forced the crowns are of no further use.

Chicory. Chicory is very much in demand as a salad. The seed is sown in late May outdoors and produces a root very much like a parsnip. The variety sown for forcing is Witloof, as this produces the tight bud needed. It must be forced in total darkness so that it becomes well blanched.

In October the parsnip-like roots are lifted and stored in sand in a frostproof shed or clamped. Do not trim off the leaves when storing or premature growth may be had. As the roots are needed they are withdrawn from the store and then trimmed to within ¾ in. of the crown and the end of the root cut back to a uniform length of 7 or 8 in.

When grown under the staging a trench 9 in. deep should be dug and the roots placed upright in this. The roots can be packed so that they almost touch and soil firmly packed down between them up to crown level. A good watering is then given. Above this dry soil is placed to a depth of 7 in. It is most important that this covering, into which the buds will push, should be dry and free from any decaying matter or the chicons may be spoiled. Boards placed on either side and supported with strong pegs will contain the covering soil. The roots will obtain moisture from below and the top soil must remain dry.

When the buds are 6 in. long they are ready for use. Any that push through the soil should be covered or they will green at the tips.

A few roots can be set in a large pot and another of similar size inserted over it. Do not forget to cover the drainage hole. A few roots potted up in this way every fortnight will provide a steady supply. Boxes used similarly will take a large number.

Chicory forces best at a temperature of approximately 50°F. (10°C.) round the roots but will also force at lower temperatures.

Seakale. Seakale is a great luxury and very easy to force. Obtain forcing crowns and treat them in the same way as chicory. Lift the roots and trim off any fangs; the thickest can be used for propagation in the spring. The trimmed roots are dibbled into a bed of soil made under the staging suitably darkened as for rhubarb, or large pots can be used filled with a good compost and the roots dibbled into this. On the whole a bed is the best method as the stems can be given more room. The bed must be kept completely dark as with rhubarb. One good watering at the start should see the crop through.

Seakale is cut when the stems are some 7 in. long and should be taken with a thin slice of the root to prevent the stem falling apart.

Mint. Roots can be dug up from the garden in December or January and laid in boxes filled with a good compost. The boxes should be 3 or 4 in. deep and the roots laid out and covered with a little soil pressed firm and level. If the box is placed in a warm place in the greenhouse and kept watered small shoots will soon appear which will prove useful at a time when mint is difficult to obtain.

16

Fruits in the Greenhouse

It is not always realised by the greenhouse owner that fruit can be grown very successfully under glass, even a cold house will often produce fruit of better quality than can be grown outdoors. Apples, cherries, figs, pears, plums, gooseberries, red and black currants are fruits which can all be grown in large pots standing outdoors for much of the year. The pots are brought into the greenhouse in February and so of course because of the earlier start earlier cropping results. After cropping the pots can be stood outdoors in order to ripen wood and buds, and left out until the following early spring. Good drainage is essential and the compost should consist of a really good turfy loam together with some opening material. Careful attention to pruning and pest and disease control must be practised as fruits under glass are very susceptible to attack by aphis, red spider and mildew.

Years ago many stately homes had orangeries, in which were grown various citrus fruits and possibly camellias. They were usually ornate long glass fronted structures built in an east west direction and the plants were grown in tubs or planted in the open border. Today we regard the larger type of greenhouse as the most suitable structure in which to grow fruit. A three-quarter span house with the wall facing south provides a good spot in which to plant fruit trees.

Apricots. This fruit should always be grown cool; it requires plenty of ventilation and in its early stages of growth a temperature maximum of 45°F. (7°C.) should not be exceeded by night or the blossom may drop off. After the fruit has stoned, i.e. formed a kernal or a seed the temperature may rise a little but the house should never be closed right up and on sunny days syringing of foliage and soil should be practiced to discourage red spider and maintain

some soil humidity. Liquid feeds can be given as the fruits swell.
During the growing period never allow the soil to become dry
but at blossom time and when fruits are ripening syringing of the
foliage should cease, though damping down of the floor should
still be done on sunny days.

The best type of tree is fan trained and it can be supported on
horizontal wires fixed at intervals and standing 6 to 10 in. out
from the back wall or the wires can be fixed to uprights where the
tree is not against a wall. Pruning is done mainly in the summer
and consists of pinching young growth back to encourage the
formation of spurs and of the retention and tying in of some young
shoots for extension and filling in. Unwanted shoots can be
removed in the autumn when the tree is retied for the following
season. Trees are best planted in October in deeply dug strong
soil and rubble may be added for extra drainage and to supply
lime.

A useful variety for the greenhouse is Moorpark. It is self fertile.

Fig. This is a rewarding fruit to grow under glass, and two or
three crops in one year are possible. The first is a terminal crop on
the previous year's shoots, the second is produced on the current
season's laterals and the third on sub laterals. However this means
a very early start in the year and minimum night temperature of
60°F. (15°C.) are required in late December and January. Without
this very early start the third crop may not ripen but be too large
to overwinter for the following spring. Therefore many growers
may decide to aim at two crops and to start their plants into
growth in late January or early February.

The fig is a vigorous tree and is best grown in large pots so that
roots are restricted and this will limit the vigour. Good drainage
is essential and some mortar rubble should be added to the compost. Every two or three years the pot should be given a little lime.
When in active growth the plants require plenty of water but this
should be limited as the crop ripens or the fruits may split. Damping down the floor and foliage except at ripening times will help.

Pruning consists of the removal of unprofitable wood, remembering that much fruit is carried on the shoot tips and provision must
be made for their replacement. Therefore one cannot spur back
growth but much must be left full length, always remembering
that the tree must be open and of good shape. Some thinning of
fruit is desirable and it is best done when the developing fruits

are the size of a pea. On average allow about three fruits per shoot. Ventilation should be given in all suitable weather. Wasps are rather fond of ripening figs and so you may require to place some wasp-proof netting over fruit or ventilators and doors. The easiest method is to make little bags of old nylon stocking and tie over the fruit. If you wish to propagate your own trees then August cuttings will root quite easily in an open mixture and under shady conditions. Brown Turkey is a good variety to grow under glass.

Grapes. Many amateurs long for a grape vine in their house and room can often be found for them in a mixed house by training one or two rods—as the long stems are called—across the north end. In this way the foliage will not shade the rest of the house. Grapes can be grown in a cold house but a little warmth will give much better results. The plant can either be planted in a greenhouse border or, as was popular in years gone by, outside the house with the trunk taken into the house through a suitable hole in the wall. Good drainage is absolutely essential and one is advised to dig two or three feet deep adding mortar rubble if needed. Never plant vines in low spots as in winter the water table may rise. Add plenty of organic manure and some bone meal before planting. The vine succeeds well on soils overlaying chalk.

Vines should be planted in a greenhouse in January. They should be well firmed and after planting given a three inch manure mulch. If more than one plant is put in space them three or four feet apart for single rods, wider for two or more rods per plant. In a lean-to or three-quarter span house plant about eighteen inches from the front wall. Eventually the rods will go up the front and the roof and finish at the back of the house though other schemes of planting can be used. The rods are supported on suitable wires about 18 in. from the glass. Soon after planting growth should be shortened to about 18 in.

In the first year train the leading shoot up as far as it grows and stop the laterals when they have made about 2 ft. of growth. Growth must be encouraged by adequate soil and atmospheric moisture coupled with as much ventilation as will keep the atmosphere buoyant. Dryness will contribute to mildew. After one season's growth the main leader is cut back by a half or to ripened wood and the laterals cut back to one bud which means close to the main rod. In two years the leader should reach the top and subsequent winter pruning consists of cutting back all lateral

growth to one or two buds or eyes. When these shoot in spring the
best growth from each fruiting spur is retained and the remainder
rubbed out in order to produce strong lateral growth. Fruit is borne
on these shoots and they should be stopped two leaves past the
flowers. Sub-laterals are stopped at one leaf. Don't be impatient,
allow no fruit to form in the first year and only a few bunches in
the second year from planting. In order to get even breaking all
along the rod the top half of the rod should be untied and allowed
to hang down. This encourages growth low down and when all
spurs are shooting evenly the rod can be retied in position.

After flowers have set and initial swelling takes place the fruit
seems to stand still for a short period at about currant sized stage.
This is the stoning period and the gardener must not allow the
plant to get a shock at this time, dryness or draughts should be
avoided. After stoning swelling is resumed and in a short while
some of the fruits must be thinned out, particularly in the centres
of the bunches. Pointed scissors called vine scissors are used for this
process (Fig. 45).

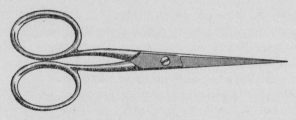

Fig. 45. Vine scissors for thinning out young grapes

The grape vine must always be grown in a buoyant atmosphere or
mildew may result. Sulphur or Karathane are good controls though
good growing must always be the first line of defence against
disease. Another common disorder of grapes is called "shanking".
This is a physiological disorder and is due to overcropping, under-
feeding, poor drainage or other improper growing.

Black Hamburgh is a very good variety to grow and it succeeds
quite well in a cool or hot house. In more favoured districts or
warm situations it will also succeed in a cold house.

Melons. The melon is one of the most luscious fruits of the garden
and is grown in a greenhouse to provide supplies from May
onwards or for later fruiting from July until September. Provided

the necessary temperature can be maintained the seed can be sown as early as January but most amateurs will be content to wait until March or even April and treat the melon as a summer crop when for the greater part of the growing period fire heat can be dispensed with, although the fruits will not be available so early in the season. Ideally the temperature of a melon house should be in the region of 65 to 70°F. (19 to 21°C.) with a minimum night temperature of 50°F. (10°C.). General cultivation is much the same as for cucumbers but the melon will prefer a rather less steamy atmosphere and fertilisation must take place before the fruits will form.

Propagation will follow the same lines as for cucumbers (see Chapter 13) the seeds being sown in 3 in. pots and pressed sideways into a light compost some four or five weeks before the anticipated date of planting out. When sowing select the fattest seeds. As soon as the seeds germinate the seedlings must be given full light but shaded from direct sun, but a high temperature is still necessary until the first true leaves have formed.

When the plants are some four inches high and the roots running freely they must be repotted into 5 in. pots using the J.I.P.2 or a similar mixture. Syringe the plants over daily with aired water and give some support as they grow. Keep the soil nicely moist but never over-water.

Meanwhile a bed must be prepared. This again can be similar to that described for the cucumbers. Mounds of prepared soil are placed on the staging and the plants trained on horizontal wires. A spacing of 18 to 24 in. should be allowed between the plants and when planting see that the top of the soil ball is well above the surface of the bed. Melons are even more prone to stem canker than cucumbers and special care is necessary to ensure that water does not hang round the base of the stem. The bed must be nicely warm before planting is undertaken. Tie each plant to a cane until it reaches the wires.

It is usual to allow the plant to grow on unchecked until it reaches the wires. The tip is then pinched out. This encourages the laterals or side shoots to grow out and which, as they grow, must be tied in to the wires. It is on these laterals and sub-laterals that the flowers will be produced. Once the fruits have set the growing point of the fruit bearing lateral should be pinched out two leaves beyond the fruit and non-bearing laterals four to five leaves from the main stem. Any shoots that develop after the crop of fruits have set must be stopped just beyond the first leaf or cut out entirely, otherwise the space will become crowded with a mass of small leaves.

Unlike the cucumber, melons will not produce fruit unless the female flowers are fertilised. The female flowers bearing the tiny knob-like embryo just behind the flower is easily recognised. Pollination can be effected in various ways. A male flower can be picked off and after removing the petals placed on the female flower so that the pollen will fall on the stigma of the latter. A soft camel-hair brush or a rabbit's tail can be used to transfer the pollen. The flowers should be fully open and as many as possible pollinated at the same time. If one flower is pollinated one day and another a day or two later the first will provide a large fruit at the expense of any others, which will be very undersized. Pollina-

Fig. 46. A female melon flower. The embryo fruit is seen just behind the flower

tion should be carried out on a warm and dry day and over this period both watering and syringing should be lessened. By picking off the earliest flowers if only one or two are ready, and waiting another day or two, a satisfactory set will be had (Fig. 46).

When it is seen that the fruits are set and beginning to swell the number should be reduced to three or four and any others removed. Those left should be distributed over the plant as far as possible. Further fruits that may form should also be removed. Once the fruits start to swell a more humid atmosphere must again be maintained and the bed kept moist. Spraying may have to be done twice a day and the floor damped down. During hot and sunny weather more ventilation will be needed and possibly some shading, but ventilators and door should be closed in good time to conserve warmth during the night. The growing melons must be supported by means of a net suspended from the wires (Fig. 47).

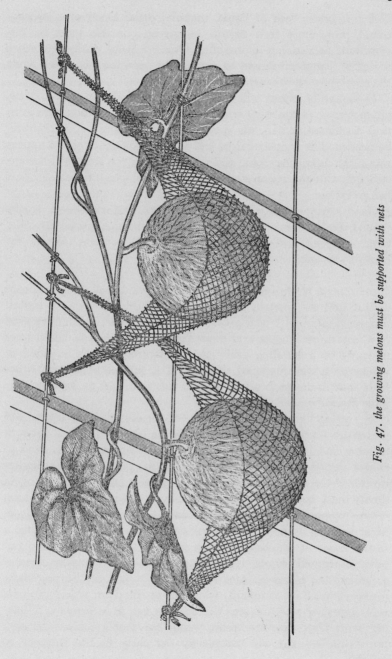

Fig. 47. the growing melons must be supported with nets

A fortnightly feed of liquid manure, dried blood or a concen-trated proprietory feed should be given, but this must be dis-continued as ripening approaches. Once or twice during growth a mulch of loamy soil should be given. The need for this is seen when the roots show on the surface of the bed.

A change of colour will indicate that maturity is near and the characteristic melon scent will be noticed. A drier atmosphere must now be aimed at and less water given and more ventilation will be needed. The fruit should be left on the plants until cracks appear round the top of the melon near the stalk and the scent will become stronger. Cut the melon and place in a cool place for some hours before eating.

Good varieties for the greenhouse are Superlative—a scarlet fleshed fruit; Hero of Lockinge—white fleshed, and Emerald Green—greenfleshed. King George (scarlet) is very suitable for cooler cultivation.

Peaches and Nectarines. These fruits respond well to greenhouse culture and the amateur gardener who produces peaches is indeed a popular person. A well grown fan-trained tree on the back wall of a lean-to greenhouse and covering say 12 ft. by 6 ft. could have upwards of a hundred fruit on it. Planting should be done in winter on a well prepared site, and it is important as with other fruit that drainage is good, and to this end and to provide lime some mortar rubber can be added.

In spring some cutting back of newly planted trees will encourage branching and these should be loosely tied to a network of wires behind the tree. Always bend over upright shoots so as to ensure a good bottom cover. It is easy to get plenty of shoots higher up. Until the area is covered some extension growth and filling in shoots must be allowed but eventually a semi-permanent branch system supporting a network of fruiting shoots should be achieved. Most training is done in the spring and summer by selecting a strong shoot at the base of each fruiting shoot and rubbing out other unwanted shoots, remembering always to consider further extension and filling in. After the fruit is picked the fruiting shoot (some 15 to 18 in. in length) is cut off at the point where the new replacement shoot starts and this shoot is tied in to fruit the follow-ing year. Over-vigorous breast wood and shoots behind the sup-ports are best cut out completely—as early in the summer as possible.

As with other fruits the peach when in growth must not be allowed to become dry at the root and syringing the foliage and damping down of the floor should be practised. Blossom and ripening fruit should not however be syringed though the atmosphere must not be allowed to become dry. When blossom is out, hand pollination—using a rabbit's tail or a brush—should be carried out. Thinning should be done over a period, some before stoning but the greater stress should be laid on the final thinning done after stoning. Stoning occurs when the young fruit is about the size of a hazel nut and at this stage there is often a considerable natural drop of fruit. Final thinning should space fruit about nine inches apart.

The peach is very susceptible to attack by red spider but the maintenance of a humid atmosphere in sunny weather does much to limit an attack. A systemic insecticide containing Rogor gives a good control, though it should not be used within seven days of picking the fruit. Aphis can also be very troublesome and this should be controlled at the first appearance of the past.

Hales Early and Peregrine are two very good varieties of peaches for greenhouse work, and Lord Napier is an excellent nectarine to use.

Strawberries. Strawberries can be picked at a very early date when grown in the greenhouse and even in a house stocked with other plants, room can often be found for a few pots, especially if a shelf is available.

Very early runners from vigorous and healthy maidens should be purchased or layered direct into small pots filled with a suitable compost. When rooted they must be removed and grown on for a few weeks in a partially shaded position. During October the plants are re-potted into the larger pots in which they will be forced. A 5 or 6 in. pot filled with the J.I.P.3 is a suitable compost, but the pots must be clean and well drained. Potting must be firm and the crown left just above the soil and the pots then stood on a bed of ashes in a frame. Remove the light as soon as the plants are re-established and only re-cover during rain or very hard weather. While in the frame do not neglect to water if necessary (Fig. 48).

The first batch of plants should be taken into the house during January where a temperature of 50°F. (10°C.) is high enough to start with but this can soon be raised to approximately 60°F. (15°C.) though the night temperature should not exceed 50°F.

(10°C.). A fairly humid atmosphere is needed and an occasional spraying over with aired water will be helpful on bright days. Do not over-water the pots but be sure that they do not dry out.

As soon as the plants show signs of flowering a weekly feed of liquid manure should be given. It is advisable to hand pollinate the flowers when they are fully open and at this time rather more ventilation can be given but be sure to avoid a draught. The temperature at this time can be increased somewhat both during the day and at night. Feeding must cease as soon as the fruits start to colour. Seven or eight fruits per plant would be a good crop and where too many flowers appear the smaller ones should be removed.

Suitable varieties for forcing are a good strain of Royal Sovereign or Cambridge Favourite (Fig. 48).

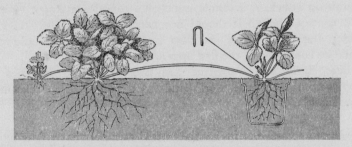

Fig. 48. Layering a strawberry runner in a 3 in. pot to ensure early and well rooted plants. The stolon is pinned down to the compost to assist rooting

UNUSUAL FRUITS IN THE GREENHOUSE

There are several fruits that are sometimes grown, largely for interest and often as a result of young members of the family sowing seed after the Christmas festivities.

Avocado or Alligator Pear. This is a stove evergreen shrub and does require high temperature. In summer 75 to 85°F. (24 to 29°C.) and in winter 55 to 65°F. (12 to 18°C.) should be aimed at. Seed is sown in spring in an open peaty compost in a temperature of up to 85°F. The seedlings are potted off in a peaty compost and the pot size increased as the plant grows. Give plenty of water and syringe daily in summer but water sparingly in winter. It will be several years before the purplish fruits are produced.

Citrus Fruits. These will succeed in a much lower temperature than the Avocado Pear. They are greenhouse evergreen shrubs needing a winter minimum of 45°F. (7°C.) and a summer minimum of 55 to 65°F. (about 15°C.). Again much moisture is required in summer with little in winter. They can be raised by sowing seed ½ in. deep in spring, but cropping from seed raised plants will be uncertain and for the best plants grafting of known varieties on to seedling rootstock is more certain. The compost for growing should consist of good loam, peat, a little old cow manure and sand. Bonemeal in the compost gives a good start but feeding in the summer will be needed. Don't be in a hurry to repot citrus fruits. The pots can be stood outdoors June to September. Fruits formed one year will not ripen until the following year, so in a well grown plant fruits in two stages may hang on the tree at the same time.

Pineapples. You can grow these plants if you have a well heated house. They are really stove plants liking sun, plenty of moisture and liquid feeding in summer but little in winter. The foliage is most decorative, spiky and somewhat like a Yucca and the fruit is borne on stems that rise from the rosette of leaves. Propagation is by offshoots or you can use the tuft of leaves taken from the top of a pineapple bought in the shop. Slice it off with a little flesh from the fruit and root it in a sandy mixture in a propagating case. The pineapple will fruit in two to four years according to the conditions under which it is grown.

Tree Tomato. The egg shaped fruits of this evergreen semi-woody shrub are reddish yellow or purple when ripe. In winter it needs a minimum of 50°F. (10°C.) and a dry air or it will rot. Propagation is by seed or cuttings in spring in a temperature of 65 to 70°F. (about 20°C.). An open mixture is needed and a 10 or 12 in. pot should accommodate a grown plant. If the greenhouse is too damp in winter the plant will probably overwinter successfully in a centrally heated dwelling house.

Popular Plants in the Greenhouse

The reader must not look for an encyclopaedic list of greenhouse plants; such a list would need several volumes of this size. Those given are amongst the most popular and better known subjects for the greenhouse and are within the skill of the keen amateur able to provide the necessary conditions. A less extensive list permits at least a brief description and short cultural notes while those plants that have a special appeal are discussed at greater length under separate headings.

The letters after the names of plants refer to the class of house best suited to their requirements, viz :

C—Cool house
T—Temperate house
S—Stove-house

It will be realised that considerable latitude can be allowed and many plants that will be happiest in a temperate house will still do quite well in the somewhat lower temperature of a cool house and vice versa.

ABUTILON T. Several species of these ornamental shrubby plants can be had and are noted for their mottled foliage and veined, bell-like and pendulous flowers. Some species are useful for training up pillars or along purlins. *A. insigne* with its rich carmine flowers is recommended for this purpose. *A. thompsonii* with large green and yellow leaves and orange carmine flowers, Red Gauntlet and Royal Scarlet are largely used as decorative plants in the greenhouse and often in conjunction with outdoor bedding schemes in the summer. *A. savitzii* has small green and white leaves.

Any pruning and trimming should be done in February, and in March repotting can be undertaken. Good drainage is necessary and ample water during the summer, but little in winter. Large specimens will need a 10 in. pot or a small tub. Equal parts of good loam, peat and leafmould plus coarse sand makes a good compost. A temperature of about 50°F. (10°C.) is ideal.

Propagation is normally by means of cuttings of side shoots taken during the spring or summer. Cuttings soon root if placed in a closed propagator and given a little bottom heat. Seeds can also be sown in the spring.

ACACIA (Mimosa) T. Trees and shrubs from Australia and other temperate zones. The dwarfer kinds are suitable for larger pots. The leaves are pinnate and the plants bear clusters of fluffy little yellow flowers in winter and spring. *A. dealbata* (the Australia Wattle) is a favourite and grown largely by commercial growers but it needs plenty of room. *A. drummondii* is more dwarf and bears tassels of yellow flowers. *A. armata* is another dwarf species; the flowers are rather larger and more fragrant than *A. drummondii*. The dwarfer species are much more suitable for the small house. *A. pudica* is the "sensitive plant".

Acacias are easily cultivated and during the summer should be placed outdoors with the pots plunged in ashes and kept well supplied with water. Pruning is done immediately after flowering and repotting every two or three years. The J.I.P.3 is a suitable compost. A temperature of 40 to 50°F. (5 to 10°C.) is sufficient although *A. dealbata* will succeed in a conservatory where frost can be kept out, but will of course flower later. The plants must be taken back into the house early in October.

Propagation is either from seed or cuttings. Cuttings are taken in June or July with a heel of old wood and rooted in a propagating frame. Seeds should be sown as soon as they are ripe in sandy peat.

ACALYPHA C, T and S. See page 149.

ADIATUM (Maidenhair Fern) C, T and S. These beautiful ferns with their finely divided leaves are extremely useful in the greenhouse as the foliage is available throughout the year. For the cool and temperate house *A. cuneatum* is the favourite and widely grown. *A. elegans* is very similar. Other kinds are *A. tenerum farleyense*, a very beautiful fern having large fronds on stalks 18 in. long. *A. macrophyllum* and *A. bausei* make very handsome plants but need the conditions of a stove-house.

Propagation is carried out by division in February and March. The plants need firm potting in a compost of two parts peat to one of loam plus some sharp sand. Good drainage is needed. Give shade during the summer and do not let the plants suffer from lack of water. During the winter give just sufficient to keep the compost moist.

AGAPANTHUS (African Lily) C. This is a very popular plant for the cool house or conservatory and is hardy in the milder districts of the south. *A. umbellatus* (now known as *A. africanus*) bears large umbels of a bright blue in summer on a stem some 2 ft. 6 in. long. Large strap-like leaves are sent up from the base of the plant. There is also a variety alba with white flowers and a named variety Moorcanus—a dark blue.

The plants are gross feeders and usually grown in tubs or large pots. Repot in March when necessary but never over-pot as it is better to leave them undisturbed and somewhat pot bound and feed regularly with manure water. Water freely during active growth but give little during the winter resting period.

AGAPETES S. See page 149.

AMARYLLIS BELLADONNA (Belladona Lily) C. A beautiful bulbous plant that bears rose-pink flowers during August and September. It is hardy in many gardens but it is a good plant for the cool or even an unheated house where it will flower rather earlier. The flowers are borne on sturdy and erect stems. The long and narrow leaves do not appear until the spring. Several bulbs should be planted up in a large pot during June in a lime free compost containing plenty of decayed leafmould and a little old manure. The bulbs should be placed well down the pot.

ANNUALS IN POTS. Many of the well known annuals can be used to provide a brilliant display of colour in the greenhouse over most of the year but especially in the spring. Most are sown in early September, the seedlings pricked out into small pots as soon as they are large enough and carefully watered through the winter until being finally potted up in February or March as they become ready. Some of the smaller kinds will make a better show if three or four seedlings are placed in one pot. Phlox drummondi, viscaria, nemesia, etc. for instance. They need only cool conditions and a cold frame should be used to raise the seeds. A shelf in the greenhouse does nicely to stand them during the winter, for they must have an abundance of light and good ventilation. Great care is needed not to over-water them or damping off may occur. Watering with Cheshunt Compound or Zineb will help to ward off this trouble.

In the early spring the seedlings are potted on into larger pots using a more loamy compost. The J.I.P.2 is very suitable or a soil-less mixture can be used. As the plants grow the taller kinds will need support of some kind and thin canes or short hazel twigs can be used.

Amongst those annuals and biennials worth while as pot plants are ageratum, antirrhinums (really a perennial), calendula, annual chrysanthemum, mignonette, nemesia, salpiglossis, schizanthus (sow July), salvia, ursinia, viscaria, etc.

ANTHURIUM   S. See page 149.

APHELANDRA   T or S. See page 150.

ARISTOLOCHIA   S. See page 150.

ARUM LILY   C or T. See Zantedeschia.

ASPARAGUS   C or T. This is a decorative evergreen plant with fern-like leaves and largely grown as a pot plant. As foliage plants they are very much in demand and noted for their extremely finely divided foliage which is admirable for mixing in with bouquets and sprays. *A. sprengeri* has a trailing habit and produces growths up to 4 ft. long and is therefore an ideal plant for the front of the staging or hanging baskets. *A. plumosus* is finer and makes a delightful plant and the leaves perfect for decorative purposes. There is a dwarf variety, *A. plumosus nanus*, which can be grown in small pots.

A good loamy compost is needed especially for *A. sprengeri*. These are moisture loving plants and during the summer must never be allowed to dry out but take care not to over-water; they will not tolerate a sodden condition. During the winter water more sparingly. Some shade during the summer is necessary and the space under the staging can often be used for a few pots of this useful plant.

Propagation is done by sowing seed in February or March in a temperature of about 55°F. (13°C.), and the seedlings potted up singly into 3 in. pots. As soon as the roots are running round the pot a larger size should be given. These should be well crocked and a little charcoal added to the compost will help to keep the soil sweet. Large and older plants can be repotted in the spring and can also be divided by carefully separating the roots and the divisions potted up to form new plants.

ASPIDISTRA   C. *A. elatior* is an evergreen foliage plant with large wide leaves. There is also a variegated form *A. elatior lurida.* Aspidistras were great favourites in Victorian days as a house plant and seem to be regaining some pupularity of late. The plant needs little attention and will remain in good condition without re-potting for several years. They need a good loamy mixture and a moderate water supply. The leaves will be all the better for an occasional sponge over.

Propagation is by divisions made in March and each piece of rhizome should have a leaf or two and a few roots attached. Old plants are best repotted in March or April.

AZALEA   C and T. See page 126.

BALSAM (Busy Lizzie)   See Impatiens.

BEGONIA (Tuberous rooted)   C or T. The begonia is one of the most popular of summer plants and certainly one of the most pleasing. The family is a large one however, and blooms may be had throughout most of the year. But the most popular of all is the tuberous rooted begonia with its double or single blooms of perfect form and of almost every shade of colour except blue.

Tuberous begonias can be raised from seed or dormant tubers. Tubers can be purchased in January or February and should be started into growth by placing them in dampened peat or a mix-ture of peat and sand. The tubers should be almost buried in the box and placed in a propagating frame or in a temperature of some 55°F. (13°C.). When growth is about 2 in. high the tubers should be transferred to 5 or 6 in. pots using the J.I.P.3. A little old cow or horse manure added to the compost will be an advantage. Feeding with liquid manure will be necessary as the plants grow and the pots become full of roots.

The flowers are in clusters of three, the centre one will give the best flower, while the wing female buds should be removed. The blooms will need some support and should be tied to a thin cane or the special adjustable wires made for this purpose can be used.

Begonias like some shade and a moist atmosphere. This can be managed by keeping the staging round the plants dampened down.

After flowering water must be gradually withheld until the leaves die down. The pots can then be stored on their sides in a temperature of not less than 40°F. (4°C.). The corms can be cleaned up and re-started into growth in February.

Seeds are sown from February until April in a temperature of 60°F. (15°C.) keeping the pans heavily shaded. Prick the seedlings off 1 in. apart into pans or boxes and when large enough pot off singly into 3 in. pots and grow on until ready for the 5 or 6 in. pots. Named varieties are propagated by means of cuttings taken from the old corms as soon as sufficient growth has been made.

Begonia (Fibrous rooted). See page 127.

BEGONIA REX   C or T. These are grown entirely for the beauty of their ornamental leaves. The leaves are attractively marked with silver and light or dark green, red or purple and green, and so on in the different varieties. They are best grown in a temperature of 50 to 55°F. (10 to 13°C.) and shade should be given from bright sun for a somewhat shady position will greatly enhance the appearance of the foliage. They will do quite well under the staging providing it is warm enough.

Propagate by dividing up old plants into rooted pieces or by leaf cuttings.

BELOPERONE   T. This plant is often referred to as the Shrimp Plant. It hails from Mexico and is grown for the pinkish-brown bracts carried at the ends of the shoots which, when fully open, bear some resemblance to a shrimp. The actual flower is inconspicuous. The plant likes a temperate house but is quite successful in a more moderate temperature. The species grown is *B. guttata*. A loamy but well drained compost is needed and plenty of water must be given during the summer but little in winter.

Propagation is by means of cuttings taken in the early summer which, when rooted, should be given a 3 in. pot and later potted on to a 5 in. pot. Shoots should be pinched back regularly to

induce a bushy plant. When established feed regularly through
the summer with liquid manure.

BIGNONIA   C or T. This is a strong growing climber and only
suitable for a large house or conservatory. Trumped shaped flowers
are borne in summer. *B. Tweediana* attains a height of some
15 ft. and *B. venusta* 10 to 15 ft. The first named bears yellow
flowers and *B. venusta* orange flowers. The latter will bloom well
into the winter. The plants like plenty of light and sun and if
possible they should be planted in a greenhouse border. Syringe
the foliage daily during hot weather. Pruning is done in early
March and consists of cutting out old or weak branches and
shortening side growths that extend too far.

Propagation is by cuttings taken in spring or by layering young
shoots in summer.

BILLBERGIA   S. These are bromeliads mostly from Brazil. They have
pineapple-like leaves rising straight up from the rootstock in the
form of a rosette. The flower spikes appear during the winter and
spring and bear brightly coloured bracts just below the flower. The
chief kinds are *B. nutans* (yellow, pink and blue), and *B. speciosa*
(carmine and violet).

Billbergias need a minimum night temperature of 55°F. (13°C.)
and a moist atmosphere. Ample water is needed during the summer
but less during the winter. Any repotting should be done in the
spring using a mixture of loam, sphagnum moss and silver sand.

Propagation is by taking any offsets or suckers when repotting
and planting up separately.

BORONIA   T. Hardwooded shrubby plants of the Rue family from
Australia. They can be grown in 6 in. pots if kept dwarf but otherwise they may grow to a height of 3 to 4 ft. The stems are long and
wiry and clothed with narrow leaves. Bell shaped flowers are borne
in early spring. The best are *B. elatior* (carmine flowers in spring),
B. Megastigma (brown and yellow) and *B. drummondii* (pink).

Pruning is done as soon as the flowers are over by shortening the
shoots by two thirds. The plants are placed in the warmest part of
the house and given frequent syringing over to induce fresh growth.
Repotting is done when the shoots are some ½ in. long, a suitable
compost being two parts peat, one part fresh loam and a good
sprinkling of silver sand. Some growers prefer up to four parts of

peat. The compost should be well rammed. In July plunge the pots in ashes outdoors to well ripen the shoots but do not let the plants dry out. In October they should be brought back into the house.

Propagation is by half ripened shoots in July placed in a closed propagator. When roots have formed pot up separately into small pots. Pinch back the tips of the main shoot and subsequently those of the side shoots.

BOUGAINVILLEA T. Climbing leaf-losing shrubby plants. The small inconspicuous flowers produced in summer are surrounded by large coloured bracts that are highly decorative. The plants remain in bloom over a long period and are ideal for clothing the wall of a greenhouse or trained to wires along the roof. They can be grown in large pots but their real beauty is seen when planted in a greenhouse border. Flowering is had during the summer and autumn. The J.I.P.3 is a suitable compost for these plants. Pruning consists in cutting back shoots of the previous year's growth to within two buds in February or March.

Propagation is effected by inserting half-ripe shoots 3 or 4 in. long in August in sandy soil and placing in a closed propagating frame. When rooted place in 3 in. pots. In late autumn or early spring the young plants can be set out in a border or potted into large pots.

BOUVARDIA T. Dwarf flowering greenhouse shrubs having slender stems with small leaves and bearing terminal clusters of red, pink or white flowers in autumn and winter. The flowers are in the form of slender tubes opening at the top into four petals. President Garfield, a double pink, and Alfred Neuner, double white, are amongst the best varieties to grow.

After flowering the plant should be rested by keeping it on the dry side until late February when it can be started into fresh growth by watering the soil and syringing over the stems. Any pruning or cutting back can be done at the same time. Pinching back during the summer will ensure late flowering.

Propagate by cuttings made of young shoots two to three inches long in the late spring. These should be inserted round a well crocked 3 in. pot in very sandy soil and placed in a propagating frame with a temperature of 65°F. (19°C.). Bouvardias can also be increased by root cuttings. Thick pieces of root rather more than 1 in. long should be planted ½ in. deep in boxes of sandy soil.

BROWALLIA   C or T. Delightful pot plants and very free flowering. It is one of the few blue flowers available during the winter. *B. elata* is a half-hardy annual and can be had in two varieties— a blue and a white. *B. speciosa major* is a perennial bearing blue flowers with a white throat and a rather larger plant than *B. elata*. Both species bear flowers in great profusion.

For winter and early spring flowering sow in July and grow on in the frame until the end of September when the plants must be moved into the greenhouse. Seed for summer flowering is sown in early spring. Successional sowings will provide a display until late in the year. When flower buds appear a weekly feed of liquid manure will be all to the good.

BRUGMANSIA   T. See Datura.

BRUNFELSIA   S. See page 150.

CALADIUM   S. See page 150.

CALCEOLARIA   C. The herbaceous calceolaria rather than the shrubby is the species that must concern us for greenhouse display and much work has been done in the past to produce the large and brilliantly coloured pouches so familiar in the late spring and early summer. These are raised from seed. Shrubby kinds may also be raised from seeds, though generally speaking they are propagated by cuttings.

Many fine hybrids can be had as will be seen from any of the seedsmen's lists and some very fine F.I. hybrids are now available. To obtain really good specimens the plants must be given cool treatment throughout their growth. A weekly feed given to well developed plants until the flowers begin to open will pay dividends. Plenty of air is needed and ample water.

Seeds of herbaceous calceolarias should be sown in May or June in pans of finely sifted compost and placed in the garden frame. The J.I. seed compost is suitable, the top half inch being passed through a fine sieve. The seed is very small indeed and must be thinly scattered over the surface of the moist soil and lightly pressed into contact with the soil, but not covered. Any watering that may be needed must be done by immersing the pan almost to the rim in water until the soil is moistened right through. A sheet of glass covered with paper should be placed over the pan and removed as soon as the seeds germinate, but continue to give some shade.

Prick out into seed trays as soon as the seedlings can be handled and pot on into 3 in. pots when a root system has developed and later into 5 in. pots using the J.I.P.2. House the plants in a cool house during the winter. In February pot on into 6 in. pots. The J.I.P.2 can again be used, to which some old and sifted cow manure has been added. The tip of the central shoot should be pinched out as soon as active growth starts in the spring to induce a bushy habit.

CALATHEA (MARANTA) See page 151.

CALLISTEMON (The Bottle Brush Tree) C. This is an evergreen shrub from Australia. It bears spikes of crimson or yellow flowers near the ends of the shoots during the summer. It does best in a cool house and can be plunged outdoors after flowering but must be brought back into the house in early October. It is not a plant for a small house. Repotting in a lime free compost will only be needed every two or three years. This should be done in February or March.

Propagate from cuttings of mature shoots during March and root in a closed propagator with bottom heat. It is, however, much better to buy in a two year old plant from a nurseryman.

CAMELLIA C. These beautiful plants are not only popular for the sake of their lovely wax-like flowers but also for their glossy foliage. The flowers may be single or double varying in colour from white to pink and deep red and of perfect form. Flowers are had in the early part of the year. The size of the shrubs makes them unsuitable for the smaller structures but many amateurs succeed in growing them on for a few years and then replacing with a young plant when the older one gets out of hand.

Annual repotting is unnecessary but it should be done every third year. A good compost would be equal parts of loam, peat or leaf-mould, well decayed manure and enough sharp grit to keep the mixture open. Lime should be avoided. Repot during March when necessary, taking care to make the compost firm round the ball of soil. Little pruning is necessary except to maintain the balance of the plant. Do not allow the shrubs to dry out at the roots nor must they be over-watered; either will result in bud dropping. An occasional feed with manure water should be given. After flowering the plants can be stood outside for the summer.

C. japonica and its many hybrids are more generally grown, but *C. reticulata* and hybrids include some of the most beautiful of all the camellias. A glance at the catalogue of any firm specialising in camellias will reveal a host of varieties.

Propagation is by means of seeds, cuttings, layers or grafting, but owing to the complex conditions called for it is far better to buy in young shrubs from a nursery. The seeds may well be two years before they germinate and must be kept moist all the time, and it is some years before the resulting plants will flower.

CAMPANULA   C. These subjects are mostly associated with the open garden or the rock garden but several are useful as pot plants. *C. isophylla* has blue or white flowers and is pendulus in habit. It is therefore most useful for hanging baskets or to grow along the edges of the staging. *C. pyramidalis*—also known as the Chimney Bell Flower—bears blue or white flowers on long spikes. The seeds are sown about May and pricked off directly they can be handled and when large enough into 5 in. pots; or they can be planted out in the open in rich soil and given their final pots in the autumn or spring. A large pot will be needed and an 8 in. pot will not be too big. The flower spikes may attain a height of 5 ft.

C. isophylla is propagated by cuttings taken in the spring. Sturdy basal shoots should be chosen and struck in sandy soil in a little heat.

Several of the more compact campanulas grown in the border can be potted up in the early autumn and taken into the cool house where they will continue to flower for some time.

CANNA (India Shot)   T. The brilliant colouring of the flowers and the bronze-brown and dark green foliage makes this one of the showiest of greenhouse flowers. *C. indica* is the species that has given rise to the many varieties that can now be had.

Cannas can be propagated from seed but the hard nature of the seeds necessitates soaking for some forty eight hours in water. Sow singly in small pots in a light compost during March, placing the seeds 1½ to 2 in. deep. Germinate in a temperature of 65 to 70°F. (18 to 21°C.). The seeds germinate irregularly and slowly and as soon as they are growing away they can be potted direct into 5 or 6 in. pots. Two or three seedlings can be placed in one pot if desired but in this case an 8 in. pot should be used.

Propagation is also carried out by dividing up old roots in early spring. Old plants should be given warmth in February and well soaked. Shoots will soon appear when the plant can be repotted and any divisions taken. Separate the roots with a sharp knife. A rich loamy compost must be used and if the plants are first given a temperature as near to 60°F. (15°C.) as possible the plants will grow apace and flower in the early summer. A compost suggested is four parts good loam and one part each of peat and dried cow or horse manure plus enough sharp sand to ensure an open texture.

Keep the plants growing in a warm house but as the flower spikes push up more airy and cooler conditions can be allowed. After flowering water should be gradually withheld as the plants dry off when the pots can be stored on their sides under the staging until the following February.

CARNATION C. The perpetual flowering carnation should be grown in an airy house with plenty of headroom and it requires a sunny position. Under these conditions the plants once established will produce flowers continuously throughout the year, although there will be flush periods. During the summer a little light shading may be needed to keep the temperature down. They require plenty of ventilation and in the summer a considerable amount of water but obviously much less in winter when growth is slower. They can be grown in 6 in. pots or in raised beds on the floor of the greenhouse. In a bed the plants can be spaced at up to 8 in. by 8 in. The soil should be open and drainage must be perfect. Lime materials should be added, unless the soil is already calcareous. Support is given in pots by canes and wire hoops and in beds by a wire and string 6 in. square network strung from four corner posts. The "layers" of supporting wire and string should be at 6 in. vertical intervals. The varieties most widely grown are sports of the Sim family. It has a good habit, is prolific but is not well perfumed. Catalogues list other varieties suitable for the connoisseur.

Propagation is by cuttings. These should be taken from healthy stock grown in good light in the early months of the year. They will root easily in sand or vermiculite and should be potted off as soon as they are rooted. Always plant shallowly and never deeper than the original depth to which the cutting was inserted. When the young plant is 8 or 9 in. high the growing point should be removed by grasping the top two or three pairs of leaves and giving a sharp pull, at the same time holding the stem lower down. The resulting breaks can be allowed to flower or can again be stopped if the summer is not too far advanced. Pot on when needed. The compost should be strong and contain some lime. During the first summer pots can stand outdoors but should be brought in by late summer. A night minimum temperature of 45 to 50°F. (7 to 10°C.) is adequate. Once established in bed or pot regular feeding with a carnation manure is required. The life of a carnation plant is approximately two years.

Green fly and caterpillar can be troublesome and red spider if it gets established will cause severe checks. Carnation rust may appear; this shows as surface lesions on stems and leaves from which brown spores in vast quantities emerge. Zineb dust or spray will control rust and hand picking of affected leaves will help the control. When spraying carnations add a spreader such as soft soap (never use household detergent) as otherwise the spray will not stick.

CELOSIA   C or T. The feathery plumes of celosia add considerably to the greenhouse display during the summer and autumn. The red, crimson, orange or yellow plumes of *C. plumosa* are well known and the plants are by no means difficult to grow. *C. cristata* is the Cockscomb—the plume somewhat resembling a cock's comb in appearance.

Seeds are sown in February or March and pricked out into small pots. Repotting into larger pots must be done as needed but as these plants simply will not suffer a check repotting should be done before the smaller pot is too full of root. A suitable compost would be the J.I.P.2 or a similar mixture. A little dried manure rubbed through a sieve and mixed in with the compost would be all too good.

CEPHALOTUS FOLLICULARIS   S. This is one of the smaller Pitcher Plants and hails from Australia. It is a carnivorous plant and produces two types of leaves, some being oval while others are formed like pitchers. The pitchers are designed to trap small insects and are marked with pink on a purple base.

CHLOROPHYTUM   C or T. Plants with long green and white leaves. *C. elatum varigatum* is the species usually grown. It is a useful plant to take into the house and seems to thrive under almost any conditions. A rich loamy soil is needed and an occasional spraying over the leaves is helpful. Small white flowers are borne on long stiff stems, which also carry little plantlets.

Propagate in the spring or summer by divisions. The plantlets can also be easily rooted.

CHRYSANTHEMUM   C. See Chapter 10.

CINERARIA   C. See page 132.

CISSUS   S. Ornamental climbers grown for their attractive foliage. They are rampant growers and need plenty of room. *C. discolor* with its leaves of mottled white on base of red and green is the best to grow and to train the shoots along the roof or on trellis.

CITRUS   T. See page 172.

CLERODENDRON   See page 151.

CLIANTHUS (The Lobster Claw Plant)   C or T. This is an interesting plant noted for its brilliantly coloured pea-like flowers. *C. puniceus* is the hardiest of the two species grown and often seen on a sheltered wall of dwelling houses in the southwest of England. Elsewhere it can be grown in the cool or temperate house. *C. dampieri*—the Australian Glory Pea—is the more difficult of the two to grow and does better in a rather higher temperature. This has flowers of bright scarlet with a deep purple-black spot. It can be trained to a trellis or pillar but is most effective when grown in a hanging basket. The long trailing shoots can become a mass of bloom. Both species are summer flowering. A suitable compost is a sandy loam two parts, and one part fibrous peat plus silver sand.

After flowering the shoots should be cut well back. *C. dampieri* is often grafted on Colutea arborescens. In this case sow the colutea three weeks before the clianthus. Cuttings can be taken with a heel in the late spring.

CLIVIA   C. Handsome evergreen plants with strap-shaped leaves and lily-like flowers. It belongs to the Amaryllis family. Clivias form large plants and should be grown in pots ranging from 6 to 8 in. in diameter or in tubs. Young plants need potting on each year but mature plants can be left undisturbed for four or five years provided a top dressing of rich soil is given annually and a feed of liquid manure occasionally. The plants must have plenty of room to develop.

After flowering keep the plants warm and moist but a period of rest in the late autumn and early winter is helpful. This can be done by somewhat restricting water supplies over this period.

Increase by division after flowering is over or remove off-sets and grow them on. Plants may also be raised from seed sown in the spring but the plants are slow to come into flower and it is better to divide.

CODIAEUM (Crotons) S. See page 151.

COLEUS   C or T. These are mostly grown for their attractive and variegated foliage. They come from Java and tropical Africa and belong to the nettle family. *C. blumei* is grown entirely for its foliage —the flowers being inconspicuous. *C. thyrsoideus* has plain leaves but bears spikes of blue flowers during winter. *C. frederica* is also useful for winter flowering.

Seed of *C. blumei* is sown during February and March on the surface of a fine compost and merely pressed down to make contact with the soil. Cover the pan with glass and paper and germinate in a temperature of 60°F. (16°C.). Prick off 2 in. apart as soon as the seedlings can be handled in J.I.P.1. When the seedlings are large enough they can be potted on into 3 in. pots and later into 5 in. pots. The young plants should be pinched back when they are some 5 in. high to ensure a bushy habit. Any flowers should be pinched off and as the pots become full of roots a weekly feed should be given.

Cuttings of about 2 in. in length can be taken during the summer and early autumn and rooted in sandy soil. These will quickly root in a propagator and will provide a show well into the late autumn if given a temperature of approximately 50°F. (10°C.). Stock plants carried through the winter will provide early cuttings in the spring.

COLUMNEA   S. Hot house flowering plants principally from South America and belonging to the Gesneria family. The drooping habit of *C. gloriosa* makes it ideal for hanging baskets. The flowers are tubular in shape and will measure up to 2 in. in length. *C. gloriosa* has bright scarlet flowers with some yellow shading on the throat.

The plants are seen at their best in hanging baskets when the long trails with their gaily coloured flowers make a blaze of colour. The baskets should be lined with moss or turves and filled with a rich compost that is open and well drained. Rooted cuttings placed round the basket and fairly close together will soon grow in the warm and moist atmosphere of the stove house. Pieces of stem will root readily when taken in the early spring if struck in a sandy compost and placed in a warm and humid propagator. The plant flowers during the winter months.

CONVALLARIA (Lily of the Valley) C, T or S. Although this is a hardy plant it is also grown very successfully in the greenhouse when its delicate and sweetly scented flowers can be had at out of season dates.

Stocks for growing in the greenhouse can be lifted from a bed in the garden or purchased during the autumn and ten or twelve of the fatter crowns placed into a 5 in. pot containing an open compost. The crowns or "pips" should be just covered. The pots should be stood in the cold frame and brought into warmth in December or January. After a short time a temperature of 65 to 70°F. (18 to 21°C.) can be given but as the buds push up a cooler temperature will make the flowers last longer. The plants will still respond to a lower temperature throughout their growth but flowers will, of course, develop more slowly.

Retarded crowns can sometimes be had from a friendly grower. These will have been refrigerated and will come into flower very quickly under suitable conditions. They can be given a temperature of up to 80°F. (26°C.) and should be placed in a dark spot until the flower buds are well seen when they must be gradually given more light and less heat.

CORDYLINE S. See page 152.

CROTON S. See page 151.

CRASSULA (Rochea) C or T. Succulent plants with small tubular flowers bunched together at the tips of the growths. They are mostly of a vivid red or pink. *C. coccinea* is the most popular species and will bloom in the early summer and continue over a long period. *C. lactea* is a creamy white and will flower in the late autumn.

Propagation is by cuttings 2 or 3 in. long taken in the spring. A few of the bottom leaves must be removed and three cuttings inserted into a 3 in. pot in a sandy compost. When rooted move all three cuttings without disturbance to a larger pot using the J.I.P.2

or a similar mixture adding a little old mortar rubble. The compost must be of an open nature and the three cuttings will well furnish the pot and produce a good show of blooms.

Crassulas have thick fleshy leaves and need careful watering for they must never be too moist nor too dry.

CUPHEA   T. The best known and more usually grown is *C. ignea*. It is commonly known as the Cigar Flower. It makes a neat bushy plant some 10 in. high. The flowers are narrow and tubular in shape and of a bright scarlet colour. The flowering season is during the summer.

Five inch pots are large enough for the final potting using a good loamy compost. Prune in January and repot when new growth appears. Cuttings are taken in spring or early summer. Pinch out the growing point of the shoot when well rooted to induce a bushy habit.

CYCLAMEN   C or T. See page 133.

CYPERUS   C or T. This is a most useful plant to stand amongst flowering subjects, the ornamental grass-like foliage being highly decorative. *C. alternifolius* or the Umbrella Plant as it is often called has narrow foliage radiating in graceful curves from the top of numerous stems. It belongs to the Sedge family.

The plants like plenty of moisture and the foliage will be all the brighter if syringed over occasionally. Repotting when necessary should be done during March or April using a compost of loam two parts, one part leafmould and sharp sand. Increase by division in March.

DAFFODILS   C or T. See Narcissi page 129.

DAPHNE   C or T. Two species are suitable for greenhouse culture. *D. cneorum* is a dwarf evergreen with delightfully scented flowers. This can be grown in a cool house and flowered in late February or March. *D. mazereum* produces purplish-red flowers on the leafless twigs in January. This also has a most attractive scent.

D. cneorum can be propagated from layers or can be grafted on a seedling plant of *D. laureola*. Cuttings of daphne can also be taken during the summer and rooted under a bell glass.

A good loamy compost is needed and young plants can be accommodated in 6 in. pots. Do not over-pot and syringe over during bright weather throughout the summer.

DATURA   T. Also known as Brugmansia or Angels Trumpet. Large evergreen shrubs and only suitable for a large house. The best plants are obtained when planted out in the border. Huge pendulous flowers of white, red or yellow are borne during the summer and early autumn. The most popular species are *D. arborea*—white; *D. sanguinea*—red; *D. knightii* has large double white flowers.

Large pots or tubs are often used when a well drained and fairly rich compost is necessary. This can consist of loam, peat or leaf-mould in equal proportions and some old manure rubbed through a sieve, plus enough sharp sand to keep the mixture open.

To propagate select shoots 6 in. long and root in a propagator, giving a temperature of 70°F. (21°C.). A winter temperature of 50 to 55°F. (10 to 13°C.) is needed.

DAVALLIA   T or H. See page 193.

DIANTHUS   C. See Carnations.

DICENTRA   C or T. *D. spectabilis* is the usual species grown and is also known as Bleeding Heart. The plant is almost hardy but can be gently forced into flower in the early spring. The long racemes of tiny crimson flowers are very decorative.

Pot up dormant roots or crowns in November and keep in a cold frame until January, when they should be brought into the house. Stand them in the coolest part of the house for a week or two and then move them into a temperature of 45 to 50°F. (7 to 10°C.).

DIEFFENBACHIA   S. See page 152.

DRACÆNA   S. See page 152.

ERICA (Heather)   C or T. Heathers provide useful colour in the greenhouse during the winter and early spring. They require a compost composed mainly of peat with a little sand, and potting— which should be done in the spring—should always be firm. Water which contains lime should never be used and rain water is probably the best to use. Amongst the best varieties for winter flowering

are *E. gracilis* a rosy red and its white form *nivalis*, *E. hyemalis*—
pink. Propagation is by means of cuttings about an inch long taken
in spring from new growth and rooted in a propagating case with
bottom heat.

EUCALYPTUS (Blue Gum) C. The flower arranger will know these
foliage shrubs well and the greenhouse owner who can supply
Eucalyptus foliage can be a popular person. It can be raised from
seeds sown in sandy soil in warm conditions in spring and it is
advisable to raise new plants every year or two. The ideal foliage
is obtained from the younger plant as after a few years the foliage
shape changes and is not so attractive. The most useful species for
the greenhouse are *E. globulus* and *E. gunnii*. The second in mild
districts will succeed outdoors.

EUCHARIS (Amazon Lily) T or S. Winter and spring flowering
bulbs which require a fairly rich compost. Bulbs are potted in summer using large pots with several bulbs. Repot every four or five
years. Water freely when in full growth and syringe foliage
frequently. Liquid feeding as flower buds appear will improve the
quality. Established pots should be top dressed in spring. Colours
obtainable are white and white and yellow and propagation is by
seeds sown about half an inch deep in a sandy compost in spring
but a high temperature is required for germination. Alternatively
offsets can be potted up in June or July.

EUPHORBIA (Spurge, Poinsettia) T or S. These require a loamy
compost with good drainage. They want warm conditions, in sun
with not too much water. The Poinsettia, *E. pulcherrima,* is now
well known for its coloured bracts seen largely during the winter
months in shops. They require a warm temperature and will not
tolerate draughts. Propagation is by cuttings taken with a heel obtained from old plants which have been cut back after the bracts
have faded. Cuts can be dipped in potassium permanganate or
charcoal to limit bleeding. Under propagating frame conditions
they will root fairly easily in a sandy peat mixture. Grow on in a
peaty compost which is on the rich side and keep in a temperature
of about 60°F. (15°C.). Spring rooted cuttings may be stopped to
provide bushiness but it is now the practice to root during the late
summer and grow on single stems using several plants per pot. The
Poinsettia is a subject which responds well to a dwarfing com-

Coleus. A favourite greenhouse plant grown for its foliage. The nettle-shaped leaves are brilliantly marked with a combination of shades of red, green, yellow, purple and cream.

A crop of Sweet Corn sown in mid-April unde[r] cloches. The variety is the John Innes Hybrid

A worth while crop of tomatoes. The variety is Sutton's Harbinger.

A good head of early cauliflower. Snowball or All the Year Round are good varieties for frame or cloche cultivation.

Early beetroots are always appreciated. A globe variety is best for cloche or frame cultivation.

pound used in the compost. In late autumn and winter the bracts will develop well in a temperature of about 60°F. but when well developed they will last longer if the temperature is lowered a little. The most popular form is the red one but it may also be obtained in pink and a creamy colour and there are named strains with enhanced colour and size. Another species grown in the greenhouse is *E. fulgens*. The flowers of this species are smaller and carried on graceful stems in clusters. The treatment should be similar to that given *E. pulcherrima*.

EXACUM   T and S. A highly scented member of the Gentian family and a plant well worth growing. It can be raised from seed sown in spring using a sandy peaty compost. The plants will require feeding and will flower in the summer and autumn. The usual variety grown is *E. affine*. This is perennial and plants will be quite short. An annual variety often grown is *E. zeylaicum macranthum* which is a deeper colour and rather taller.

FABIANA (False Heath)   C or T. A useful plant flowering in May and having white flowers. The compost can be J.I.P. and any re-potting done in spring. Propagation is by cuttings rooted in sandy soil under cool conditions in spring.

FERNS   There is a wide variety of ferns which can be grown in the greenhouse, some of which require stove house treatment and are discussed in that chapter devoted to stove plants. See also Adiantum. A suitable compost for ferns consists of a mixture of mainly turfy loam with some leafmould or peat and sand. One can also add a little well rotted manure. Propagation should be done by tearing old plants apart using mainly the outer part and repotting in spring. Generally speaking moisture is required in the atmosphere but for the cool house varieties they should not receive a lot of water during the winter. Useful varieties to grow for the cool and temperate house include Asplenium bulbiferum, Cyrtom-ium the holly fern, Osmunda regalis the royal fern and Pteris cretica. Within these genera are many species worth growing but which we have no room to mention here.

FICUS (Rubber Plant, Fig)   T. This is a large family but the best known is *F. elastica* the India Rubber Plant. It requires a loamy compost and repotting should be done in spring. Not much water in winter but plenty in summer, and foliage should occasionally be syringed, particularly if any stove species are grown. Propagation is by cuttings inserted in a sandy compost in a propagating case in spring.

FRANCOA (Bridal Wreath)   C. This plant requires a loamy compost and it should be grown cool, in fact it can be in frames during the first season. Seed is sown during the spring and early summer and by the following summer the plants should have reached a 6 or 7 in. pot with 2 ft. shoots carrying clusters of flower. The usual variety grown is *F. ramosa* which is white but there are also pink and red species.

FREESIA   See page 134.

FUCHSIA   C or T. See page 122.

GARDENIA   S. See page 152.

GERANIUM   C or T. See page 120.

GERBERA (Transvaal Daisy)   C. This plant requires a well drained compost and should be given cool conditions. It will succeed outdoors in milder parts of the country although it is best to cover the plants with cloches during the winter months as any excess water in the winter resting period may tend to rot the plant. It can also be grown in a cold frame or planted in the soil in the greenhouse provided the house is cool. The main flowering period is throughout the late spring, summer and autumn and the hybrids available give a colour range from white to yellow, pink and red. The plant is herbaceous and cleaning up and removal of old leaves should take place during the late winter and early spring. It is possible to propagate by dividing the plants, but better results are achieved by sowing seed, which must be fresh as available.

GESNERIA   S. See page 152.

GLADIOLUS   C. Gladioli can be brought into flower very much earlier by using a greenhouse. Corms can be planted in the soil of the greenhouse or several may be placed in a large pot. The corm should be buried 2 to 3 in. Hybrid varieties are normally grown and early flowering corms such as The Bride, are available.

Propagation is by natural division of corms or by growing on the cormlets formed around each corm after each season's growth. The corms after flowering in the greenhouse should be well dried and stored for the following season.

GLORY PEA See Clianthus.

GLOXINIA C or T. These showy plants with their large bell-like flowers in whites, pinks, blues and reds are useful for summer and autumn display and if grown in warm conditions can be made to flower early and late. They can be raised from seed sown on the surface of a fine compost at most periods of the year although a temperature of about 60°F. (15°C.) is required for germination. The seedlings must be handled when small, pricking off by pressing into the surface of a fine compost and keeping it under closed conditions until actively growing away. The seedlings will form a corm and flower can be produced in about six months from sowing. They can also be raised from leaf cuttings. After flowering the corm should be allowed to go to rest by withholding water and rested during the winter in dry conditions at a temperature of about 50° F. (10°C.). Corms can be restarted into growth in early spring by knocking them out of the old pots and plunging in sandy peat placed in a propagating case. Once the corms have started into growth they should be potted in 5 or 6 in. pots with the corm at about soil level. We have listed Gloxinia here as it is normally known by this name but its true botanical name is Sinningia.

GREVILLEA (Silk Bark Oak). Two species of this evergreen shrub are grown; G. robusta and G. rosmarinifolia. They can be raised from seed sown in spring in a temperature of about 60°F. (15°C.) and because the shrubs may tend to go fairly tall it is best to raise fresh plants every few years. The foliage is most useful for the flower arranger and is frequently glycerined for preservation.

HEDERA (Ivy) C. Several types of ivy, particularly that with variegated foliage, is useful in a greenhouse. It can be propagated by rooting young shoots in a sandy compost.

HELIOTROPIUM (Heliotrope or Cherry Pie) C or T. A greenhouse shrub with fragrant blue or white flowers. This plant can be used for bedding out in the summer either as a bush or as a standard. It is propagated from seed sown in the spring or by cuttings of shoots obtained from cut back older plants. Cuttings can be taken in spring or late summer. Young plants should be pinched in order to encourage a bushy habit but if you require a standard then the cutting once rooted should be allowed to grow unstopped to the desired height. It should be tied to a cane. *H. peruvianum* is the species normally grown although it has many selections.

HIPPEASTRUM (Amaryllis) T or S. This handsome bulbous plant with its two foot stems crowned with two or three showy flowers is a fine sight during the spring and summer. Bulbs can be bought and they should be potted in a loamy compost during January and the bulb should be inserted about half of its depth. If placed in a temperature of 65 to 70°F. (18 to 21°C.) growth will soon start and the flower bud will elongate rapidly. The leaves will come later than the flower bud. Plenty of water is required when in growth but once the flower has faded and the leaves die down water must be withheld. During the growing season liquid manures should be given in order to build up for the following year. Resting after growth should be in a temperature of about 50°F. (10°C.). A later start in spring will simply mean later flowering. Propagation can be by seed sown in well drained pots in spring or by offsets removed from mature bulbs. Mature bulbs require repotting every three or four years but should have an annual top dress of rich compost. Hybrids are normally grown rather than species.

HOYA (Wax Flower) C or T. A beautiful climbing plant with deep green fleshy leaves. It can be grown in pots and the shoots allowed to climb purlins or prepared supports. Over-potting will limit flower production which occcurs each year from the same place on the shoot. Little water is required in the winter but a fair amount in the summer. Any repotting should be done in spring when any pruning should also be done. This consists largely of removing unwanted shoots and some cutting back in order to obtain further shoots for tying in. Propagation is by cuttings inserted in a sandy compost and given bottom heat. The usual varieties grown are *H. carnosa*, pink and white; and *H. bella* white and crimson which requires a higher temperature than *carnosa* and does not climb so well.

HYACINTHUS C or T. See page 130.

HYDRANGEA   C or T. The greenhouse owner will be mainly con-concerned with *H. hortensis* and its named varieties. The compost should consist of mainly rich loam with some well decayed man-ure and sand. The best blooms are on young plants propagated in summer. Cuttings root easily in single pots or around a pot using a sandy mixture and the pot stood in a shady frame. After potting they can be grown under cool conditions during the winter and will flower the following spring. It is however usual to pinch the young plants in spring so that vigorous shoots are produced during the summer. These will terminate in a flower bud which can be forced into flower during the spring of the following year and timing will depend on whether they are in a cool or temperate house. Any pruning for shape and shoot regulation should be done in late sum-mer by removing weak and straggly shoots. Some leaves may drop off during the winter but this is quite natural. Pink varieties respond to blue hydrangea colourants but the white and red should be grown normally.

HYPOCYRTA   S or T. This is a "new" plant and would appear to be a long suffering plant that will withstand much misuse. It is a low shrub-like plant with thick small leaves and from the axils of these leaves appear small orange-red flowers. The flowering period ex-tends for a very long time and masses of flowers are produced. Because of its thick leaves it will withstand dwelling house con-ditions well. It can be propagated by cuttings and probably the best time is the spring. *H. glabra* is the usual species grown.

IMPATIENS   C or T. This is the Busy Lizzie. An easy plant to grow and often seen indoors and the flat flowers produced over very long periods make an attractive pot plant. It requires a well drained rich soil and a temperature of about 50°F. (10°C.) seems to suit it best. The varieties *I. holstii* and *I. sultanii* and the hybrids have been grown for years and will make, in a 6 or 7 in. pot, a plant 2 ft. or more across. Little pinching or pruning is required as it branches naturally, though any precocious shoot may be pinched back to retain a good shape. Today the F.1. hybrids are more popular than the older varieties. They are dwarfer and come in a wider range of colours and produce even more flower. These F.1. hybrids make excellent bedding plants and can be raised from seed sown in the spring and it will bloom that same summer, or it can be propagated by cuttings rooted in a sandy compost

when material is available. Any dryness or over watering or starva-
tion may cause leaves to yellow and fall. Imp is a first class F.1.
hybrid variety to grow either as a pot plant or as bedding.

IPOMŒA (Morning Glory)   C, T or S. Beautiful perennial and half
hardy annual climbers. The stove species require a peaty soil and
are generally perennial and if so can be trained up trellis and any
pruning done in spring. The variety usually grown is *I. rubro-
caerulea*, Heavenly Blue. This is normally sown in spring and would
not then require stove conditions. Sow two or three seeds in a
small pot and pot on to the flowering size pot, i.e. 5 or 6 in. pot.
Support must be provided and the plant will climb of its own ac-
cord. Flowers only last for a very brief period but are produced in
quantity each day. The colour is Cambridge Blue. A perennial
variety which is a deep blue is *I. learii* and this will grow 10 or 12 ft.
high.

IRIS   C. The Iris is too well known to need description and both
bulbous rooted types and rhizomatous species can be introduced
into the greenhouse. Six or eight inch pots of the *rhizomatous I.
unguicularis* can be established and during the summer months
given full sunshine outdoors. If brought into a cold or cool house
during the winter they will produce their pale blue flowers. The
bulbous types should be potted up in 6 in. pots in August and
September using about five bulbs to a pot. The bulbs should be
covered. They can be stood outdoors until November but should
not be put in a plunge bed as is done with narcissi. If brought into
the greenhouse before Christmas and given cool conditions they
will come into flower earlier than they would outdoors. *I. tingitana*
will flower very early and the delightful miniature *I. reticulata,
histrioides* and *danfordiae* will follow in their season. The miniature Iris are better grown in pans or half pots. These can be followed by the usual garden varieties of bulbous Iris such as Wedg-
wood, Yellow Queen, Imperator and Professor Blauw—a delightful
deep blue variety. These can be potted or boxed in October and
brought into flower in the cool greenhouse in spring or they can be
planted direct in the soil in the cold or cool greenhouse in October
and November when they will flower in late March and April
according to temperature which should never exceed 50°F. (10°C.).

JACARANDA (Mimosa-leaved Ebony Tree)   T or S. This plant is grown largely for its fine foliage and it requires a peaty soil with good drainage. It can be propagated by seed sown in spring in a very warm position or by cuttings rooted in peat and sand under propagating case conditions.

JASMINUM   C. This is a beautiful scented climber and wherever possible should be included in any greenhouse. It can be kept in pots stood against a trellis or other support or planted in the border. A little old manure added to the compost will give vigour and the compost should be made open by the addition of some course sand. The foliage should be syringed over frequently and a close watch kept for any pests. It can be propagated from cuttings rooted in sandy compost. The most popular varieties are *J. officinale*, grandiflorum—white, flowering in summer; *J. primulinum*—primrose, flowering in spring and the winter flowering *J. polyanthum*, which is white.

KALANCHOE   C. This plant has deep green succulent leaves producing spikes of scarlet flowers in spring. Seed should be sown on the surface of a fine compost during spring, pricked off when large enough then moved to 3 in. pots and finally to 5 in. pots during the summer. They like a sandy compost and appreciate a little old cow manure. When once in their final pots after establishment they can stand in the frame until autumn then returned to the greenhouse. A temperature of 50°F. (10°C.) will suit them very well. The usual variety grown is *K. blossfeldiana*.

LACHENALIA (Cape Cowslip)   C. This is a bulb flower bearing short stems with tubular flowers and they bloom in early spring. New varieties have given a range of colours in shades of red and yellow. The compost should be on the open side and pots, pans or baskets can be used. The bulbs should be planted about ½ in. deep or pushed in at 2 in. intervals in the sides and top of a basket. Plant in August and leave in a cold frame until November then take into a cool airy greenhouse. During the growth period plenty of water will be required and occasional liquid feeds, but after flowering dry off outdoors to ripen the bulbs. They can be propagated from offsets removed from the old bulbs at potting time.

LILIUM   C or T. This is too big a group of plants to deal with in any detail in this book and reference should be made to one of the

many excellent books that have been written devoted entirely to
the lily. The compost for lilies should consist of loam, leaf-mould
or peat, old manure and sand and potting is done during the
winter months using one bulb in a 5 in. pot or more in a large pot.
Some varieties are stem rooting and for these deeper planting must
eventually be achieved and it is done by planting the bulb much
lower in the pot and then just covering the bulb. Later, as the
stem grows well clear of the pot further compost is placed in the
pot and the stem roots into this additional compost. After planting
the bulb can be kept in a cold frame or cold greenhouse with ash
or peat covering the pots until growth commences. They should
then be removed to the greenhouse where they will eventually
flower. During the summer months the pots can be stood outdoors.
Water freely when in full growth and give liquid feeds. If one
wishes to force suitable varieties a temperature of 55 to 60°F. (12
to 16°C.) will be sufficient. Lilies can be propagated by seeds sown
in autumn or spring in a sandy soil and grown on to flowering
size which may be from one to seven years. *L. formosanum pricei*
will flower in the first year after sowing. They may also be propagated by splitting of scales and inserting them in sandy peat with
bottom heat. Young bulbs will be formed at the base of the scales.
For varieties specialised lists should be consulted.

Lotus (Birds Foot Trefoil) T. This is an ornamental shrubby
plant about two foot high bearing scarlet flowers in summer. The
compost should be a sandy loam with some peat and sand. Repotting is done in spring and they require a light airy position in
the sun. Not a great deal of water is required, particularly during
the winter, but some liquid feed can be given during the flowering
period. *L. bertholettii* is the usual species grown. It can be raised
from seed sown in sandy soil in spring or from cuttings rooted in
a cool propagating frame during the summer.

Maranta   See page 152.

Marguerite   C. Older gardeners will remember this plant with
daisy type flowers once used for bedding, but now not so frequently seen. Propagation is by cuttings taken from plants during
late summer and autumn and they can be rooted in a shady frame
quite easily. Once rooted they should be potted up, pinched when
5 or 6 in. tall and grown on during the winter in the greenhouse.

They will have to be transferred to a 5 in. pot from which they can be planted out after danger of frost has passed in late spring or early summer. Cuttings taken in May and grown on outdoors during the summer will make large plants for flowering in the greenhouse the next spring if taken back into the house in September. Plants can be kept for two years but because of the room they take up it is probably better to root a fresh stock each autumn. They require a lot of water and plenty of feeding and a careful watch should be kept for any insect pests.

MAIDENHAIR FERN   See Adiantium, pages 149 and 193.

MIGNONETTE   C or T. A very useful plant to grow in pots. It should be sown in August or September and a cool house will carry it through the winter. The soil should be open and two or three plants can be grown in a 5 in. pot. The giant flowered selections are very sweetly scented and have a good spike quality.

MIMOSA (Sensitive Plant)   T and S. These plants have the curious habit of collapsing their Acacia-like foliage when touched and the plant can prove an interesting exhibit to those who are not aware of this habit. Two species are generally grown *M. pudica* and *M. sensitiva*. Although it is perennial it is normally grown as an annual as overwintering appears to be difficult unless dryish stove conditions are given. It can be raised easily from seed sown in early spring under stove conditions. See also Acacia.

MONSTERA   See page 153.

MUSCARI (Grape Hyacinth)   C. A very useful short bulbous plant which is easy to grow. Pot up the bulbs in autumn using pans or 5 in. pots and keep them in a cold frame until after Christmas and then bring into a warm greenhouse where they will soon flower.

MYRTUS (Myrtle)   C. This evergreen shrub is grown for its fragrant white flowers and its foliage. The compost should be a sandy loam with peat and sand and the pots must be well drained. During summer the pots can be stood outdoors when it will need plenty of water and frequent syringing of the foliage. Pruning is done in February by controlling shape and unwanted shoots. It can be raised from seed in a warm position in autumn or spring or by rooting cuttings in a sandy soil with a little bottom heat in a propagating case.

NARCISSUS   See pages 68 and 129.

NERINE   C. This is a bulbous plant often grown outdoors but which can be grown in pots. They should be given a rich soil and potted three per 6 in. pot. Potting is done in the early summer when bulbs are resting. Once growth starts keep them well watered until leaves die down the following spring. The flower appears first and will be in bloom in October and November and a cool house will be plenty warm enough. The following spring after growth has died down the pots and bulbs should be kept dry and exposed to full sunshine so as to harden them. They may be kept in the same pots for several years but top dressing is needed after the first season. Propagation is by offsets which can be separated and potted up at the normal potting time. There are several varieties with a colour range in pink, rose, scarlet and crimson.

ORCHIDS   S. In the limited space available it would be impossible to do justice to the Orchid and the reader is advised to consult works devoted to this subject for detailed information. The orchid is not a great deal more difficult to grow than many other plants but it must be given the right conditions for its type. It is best to grow orchids on their own and the structure of the greenhouse and the temperature which can easily be maintained must decide the species which you can grow. The greenhouse must be well constructed and ventilation provided not only along the ridge but also low down so that fresh air can be led in after first passing over the pipes and then stale air will make its way via the ridge. Any badly fitting ventilators or doors which could conceivably give rise to a draught when winds are strong are fatal to orchid growing. A house devoted to orchids should have an earthen floor and benching above the level of the wall ventilators. A solid wall of brick is desirable. Houses can be divided and heating arrangements varied so that areas of differing temperatures can be available. Provision must also be made for shading, preferably of a roller type because during summer orchids will require shade from the time when the sun shines on the house until it leaves it, but in winter shading is often not required at all. Orchids have a resting period and as far as possible the rest should take place during the winter months when, generally speaking, much less water is required though with those orchids which do not make bulbs or which keep growing all the time some water is required during this resting period. Nowadays most composts are based on osmunda fibre and varying quantities of sphagnum peat and old crushed pots for drainage are mixed in. The orchid must have perfect drainage and so the pot is usually crocked for a quarter of its depth. Potting and re-potting is done as far as possible in the spring and bulbs are not covered. The compost instead of being firmed with the fingers should be pushed down with a potting stick so that horizontal strands of compost are avoided.

If you are going to start with orchids the following will succeed in a cool house with a winter night minimum of 45°F. (7°C.). *Cymbidium* and its hybrids, *Cypripedium insigne* and its hybrids, *Odontioda* and *Odontoglossum*. If you wish to grow the *Vandas,* the *Dendrobiums* and the *Cattleyas* temperate, and in some cases, stove conditions will be needed.

PALMS C T and S. These are decorative plants of great value for all types of greenhouses. Some attain noble proportions making them suitable for large greenhouses and conservatories, while others when small are ideal for the small house or even for table decoration.

Areca lutescens is a good palm to grow. Its yellow stems add interest to the plant. Although it can become a very large plant it can also be grown in a 5 or 6 in. pot and is suitable for a warm house. *Chamaerops humilis* is useful for the temperate house and known as the Fan Palm. The leaves are fan-shaped with spiny stalks some 3 ft. long. *C. fortunei* is also largely grown. Amongst the most useful of the palms and very popular are *Kentia belmoreana* and *K. forsteriana* (syn. Howea), and will do quite well in a cool house. As small plants these palms are extensively used for table decoration and as larger specimens for the greenhouse and conservatory.

A suitable compost for palms consists of one third fibrous loam, one third leafmould or peat and one third sand; crushed brick is often included in the compost. A well drained and open compost is needed. Palms must never be overpotted and a move into a larger pot is only made when the old pot becomes full of roots. A good supply of water is essential but it must never be overdone. In winter the supply must be lessened but the soil must still be kept moist.

Syringe the plants over regularly during spring and summer and occasionally sponge the leaves to remove dust, etc.

Propagation is by seeds but in the ordinary way it does not pay to do this as it is far better to buy in young plants and grow them on. This saves a year or two of waiting.

PASSIFLORA (The Passion Flower)   C or T. There are several kinds of this showy climber suitable for greenhouse culture one of the best being *P. coerulea*, blue. A hybrid Constance Elliott, white, and another hybrid *P. Allardia* bears almost pure white flowers with a pink flush. *P. racemosa* has red and white flowers and *P. coccinea*, red.

The plants are grown in large pots or tubs or, where there is ample room in the border. Repotting of small plants is carried out in February or March. The pots or tubs must be well drained and the compost can be of fibrous loam, three parts, peat one part with some sharp sand.

Pruning is done during the winter and consists in cutting out any weak or unwanted growths back to two eyes and retaining other growths to fill the space available without overcrowding.

Propagation is by cuttings taken in the spring. Shoots about 5 in. long with a heel are needed and should be inserted in a sandy mixture and covered with a bell glass or placed in a propagating frame.

PELARGONIUM   C or T. See page 119.

PHILODENDRON   S. Evergreen climbing plants from the forests of tropical America. They have ornamental foliage and flowers in the form of spathes which are of various shades of purple, red, pink or white. In their wild state they twine their slender stems amongst the branches of trees.

P. scandens is the species usually grown and needs moist and warm conditions if it is to succeed. A compost of equal parts loam and peat plus coarse sand is suitable. The plants produce aerial roots and if given the support of a pole covered with moss or branches to which the roots can adhere the plant will be supported. These interesting plants are by no means difficult to grow but they need a high greenhouse.

Propagate by pieces of stem with several joints. These soon root in a warm propagating frame. Layers can also be rooted.

PLUMBAGO (Leadwort) C or T. Climbing leaf-losing shrubs that bear blue flowers in summer. Plumbago can be grown in a large pot or tub but it is another shrubby plant that is better given a place in the border. The favourite kind is Plumbago capensis. This has light blue flowers and will go on blooming over a long period. There is also a white form. Prune after flowering.

POINSETTIA T. The popular name for Euphorbia pulcherrima which is grown for its scarlet bracts and which are in full beauty during the winter. See Euphorbia.

PRIMULA C. See page 136.

POLYANTHUS C. See pages 69 and 138.

ROSA C or T. Roses can be grown in the greenhouse border if room permits but most gardeners will prefer to grow them in pots for in this way the room they would occupy can be given over to other plants during the summer and autumn.

Young plants should be obtained in October and potted into 7 or 8 in. pots. Remove the old soil from round the roots and trim back any that are damaged. After crocking the pots half fill them with the compost and stand the plants on this with the roots well spread out. Complete the filling, working the soil well in between the roots and firming. Chopped turfy loam five parts, peat one part and old manure one part with some sharp sand will make a suitable compost.

After potting the plants should be stood outdoors until December when they can be pruned and taken into the house. This pruning should be severe and growths should be cut back to two or three buds and any weak growths removed. Only a moderate temperature should be given the first year and the plants syringed over daily. When growth is active a feed of weak manure water should be given at intervals. Blooms should be had during April in a cool house.

After flowering stand the plants outside and plunge them up to the rims in ashes. On no account allow the roots to become dry during the summer. Repot in September and return to the plunge bed until December when they must go back into the house.

After flowering again stand the plants outside and plunge to the rims in ashes.

Pruning is carried out a week before housing and the extent will now depend largely on the type of growth, but normally a strong growth should be cut back to the fourth plump bud and less robust growths to two buds. Take out any weak growths. During the second year rather more heat may be given and blooming should be had at a rather earlier date.

There are plenty of suitable varieties to choose from. Hybrid Teas are very suitable and Madame Butterfly, Hoosier Beauty, Richmond, Golden Ophelia, Sylvia and Roselandia are but a few. A climbing rose can be used to clothe the wall of a lean-to; Marechal Niel or Golden Ophelia are splendid for this purpose.

SAINTPAULIA (African Violet) T. A plant for the warm greenhouse. It is a charming little plant some 4 in. high with fleshy ovate leaves. The flowers are a deep violet-purple not unlike a violet and have bright yellow stamens. They are very popular as house plants but unless given the right conditions they soon fail.

Careful watering is essential and the plants are happier if they are stood on a shallow pan filled with finely broken brick. The brick rubble is kept watered and this is absorbed by the compost in the pot and no water is given otherwise. Too dry an atmosphere must be avoided and also draught. Never water over the leaves. The compost recommended is two parts fibrous loam and one part each of leaf-mould and peat plus a little sand or a good sample of J.I.P.2 will serve. The plants are flowered in 3 in. pots.

Propagation is normally by way of leaf cuttings but the plants can be raised from seed. Leaf cuttings must be placed in a propagating frame.

S. ionantha is the only species but there are now a number of named varieties, some of which are double.

SANSEVIERIA T or S. These are popular as house plants but are better grown in a warm greenhouse. The most popular species is *S. trifasiata* and there are several varieties. The leaves are sword shaped 1 to 2 ft. in height and pointed at the ends. They have light and dark green mottling and some have yellow bands round the leaves. It is an easy plant to grow but very little water will be needed during the winter.

Propagation is by offsets or suckers. Leaf cuttings will also root in a propagating case. A light sandy soil is needed.

SCHLUMBERGERA C or T. This is still more generally known as Zygocactus truncatus or the Christmas Cactus. It is a favourite greenhouse and room plant. It has flattened and thick drooping stems much jointed and very branching and bears terminal flowers of pink or white. There is another form known as the Easter Cactus which bears red flowers in the early spring. Christmas Joy is yet another form and is salmon in colour. Blooms will be had from October onwards. Both of these forms are rather more upright in habit than the Christmas Cactus.

Little water is needed from October to March but in April the plants should have a good soaking and after that kept nicely moist during the summer. The great thing to remember is that it will not suffer a badly drained soil. Some shade may be needed while the young growth is tender but otherwise the plants will revel in full sun. This will do much to bring about abundant flowering in winter.

Stock is easily increased by breaking off two or three inches of a stem at a joint and inserting in sandy soil. Two or three cuttings should be placed in each pot

SOLANUM C or T. *S. capsicastrum*—the Winter Cherry—is the more usually grown of this genus but it contains both climbing and dwarf species. *S. capsicastrum* makes a fine plant for winter in the greenhouse and its green foliage and red berries are very welcome during the dark days.

Seed is sown in February or early March in a temperature of about 60°F. (16°C.) and the seedlings pricked out 1½ in. apart as soon as they can be handled. The J.I.P.1 is suitable. Before any overcrowding occurs pot on into 3 in. pots and when 3 in. high pinch out the centre to induce a bushy habit. In early June pot on into 5 in. pots and in a few days transfer to a frame or plunge in ashes. The light should be left off except during hard rain. Pinch the shoots back again in June or July.

Frequent syringing over with water is needed when the plants are full of bloom. This will help the flowers to set for on this will depend the show of ripe berries in the winter. At the end of September the plants should be well covered with berries and can be taken into the greenhouse where they will ripen.

STEPHANOTIS S. See page 154.

STRELITZIA   S. See page 154.

STREPTOCARPUS (Cape Primrose)   C or T. These showy and fascinating perennials have been greatly improved over the last few years and a good strain of modern hybrids will provide a wealth of flowers in a wide range of colours. A fairly high temperature is needed to start with but once the initial stages are over cool treatment is needed.

The seed is very small and careful sowing is very necessary. Sow in a well drained 5 in. pot or a pan in January making sure that the surface of the compost is very fine and only give the merest covering with fine sand or simply press the seed on to the compost. Prick out at 1 in. apart as soon as the seedlings can be handled in a light compost and when sufficiently large prick out separately into 3 in. pots using the J.I.P.1 or a similar mixture.

Stand the pots in the warmest part of the house and when well rooted repot into 5 or 6 in. pots using the J.I.P.2. Do not make the compost too firm but just lightly press it round the plants with the fingers. Keep the compost moist but never overwater. Give ample ventilation and keep cool. As soon as any sign of flowering is seen start a weekly feed.

Seed is also sown in July and the seedlings overwintered in the house in 3 in. pots. A temperature of 45°F. (7°C.) is desirable but a degree or two less will not matter. In March move into 5 or 6 in. pots and grow on in a cool temperature. July sowing should give flowers in early summer the next year, while a January sowing will give flower from August onwards.

The plants can be kept for two or three years and old plants can be divided to increase the stock, but it is better to sow seed.

STREPTOSOLEN   T. *S. jamesonii* is a very free flowering plant and bears clusters of orange coloured flowers in the spring and early summer. It makes an excellent pot plant or can be allowed to climb. It needs a good rich compost and for pots it should be pinched back several times but the plant is seen at its best when grown as a climber. It is sometimes trained as a standard.

Pruning is done immediately after flowering when the shoots should be cut back fairly hard. It is propagated by cuttings of young shoots taken during the early summer and rooted in a propagating frame.

TRADESCANTIA C or T. Greenhouse and hardy perennial plants. Zebrina pendula is particularly useful for draping along the edges of the staging or for hanging baskets. Zebrina has silvery green leaves and central band and stripes of reddish-purple. *T. reginei* is similar in habit but more delicate—the leaves having a purplish flush over light and silvery-green.

Pieces of stem of any length will easily root if pushed into a little soil. If given too much shade the leaves are apt to lose their attractive colouring and become quite green.

TRITONIA C or T. Closely allied to the Montbretias these bulbous plants make a good show on the greenhouse bench during May and onwards. The bulbs should be potted up in November placing five bulbs in a 5 in. pot filled with a good loamy compost. The pots can stand in the cold frame until growth is well advanced when they should be brought into the greenhouse and given a cool position.

Annual potting is not recommended as they seem to do better if left undisturbed for three or fours years. Increase by offsets or seed. *T. crocata* is usually used for pots. The variety Prince of Orange has orange-scarlet flowers and Salmon King has flowers of a pretty salmon shade. These are borne on long wiry stems.

TULIPA See page 131.

VALLOTA (Scarborough Lily) C. A bulbous plant somewhat similar to a small Hippeastrum. Scarlet flowers are carried on long stems in the late summer. The bulbs should be potted singly into 5 in. pots or three can be planted in a 7 in. pot during late October or early November. A good loamy compost is needed and the bulbs should be planted so that the tops are seen just above the compost. Moisten the compost and stand in a sunny position in the house and give a little water until growth is seen. The strap-like leaves are retained throughout the season. Do not repot for several years, but established plants should be given feeds of liquid manure.

When repotting becomes necessary it should be done during March. *V. purpurea* is the only species worth growing.

VERONICA C. There are several veronicas that are useful for a cool house. Most will bloom during the autumn. *V. speciosa* is largely grown and varieties can be had in shades of rose, red, mauve, pink and blue. *V. hulkeana* is used for pot work and its lovely panicles of lilac flowers can be enjoyed during the spring.

Stock can be increased by cuttings in August. Insert partly ripened cuttings in sandy soil and stand in a cold frame. Pot off when well rooted and pinch back the centre of the plant to induce a bushy habit. Move into a cool house in the late autumn. Established plants should be stood outdoors during the summer.

ZANTEDESCHIA C or T. Better known as the Arum Lily. The actual flowering time largely depends on the temperature that can be given. In a temperate house blooms should be available during March. The Arum Lily *Z. aethiopica* is white and grows about 2 ft. high. A yellow species is *Z. elliotiana* and has dark green leaves spotted with white. In a cool house flowering will be a little later but the plants will do quite well even in a cold house in many parts of the country.

After flowering the plants should be gradually dried off and rested with the pots laid on their sides until early August, when those needed for early flowering must be repotted. For later flowering late August or early September will serve. A compost of four parts loam, one part leafmould or peat and a little old manure plus some sharp sand is recommended. A small handful of bonemeal can be added to the compost with advantage. Old cow manure was once favoured by growers.

After repotting the plants should stand outdoors and be kept nicely moist until early October when they must be housed. When the roots are running freely round the pots a regular feed should be given. Keep the foliage syringed over and watch out for greenfly.

Propagation is by offsets taken when repotting.

ZEBRINA C or T. See Tradescantia.

ZONAL PELARGONIUM (Geranium) C or T. See Pelargonium, page 121.

ZYGOCACTUS C or T. See Schlumbergera.

WHAT CAN GO WRONG?

Many of the pests or diseases that may attack our plants will already be familiar to the gardener but some are more peculiar to plants grown under artificial conditions of climate and environment. When a plant is not growing normally one must not immediately think that it is attacked by some pest or disease. Though this may be the case many troubles are physiological and are caused by conditions or soil which do not suit the plant in question. A well grown plant is more likely to resist disease than one which is constitutionally weak and good cultivation and strict hygiene must always be the first line of defence. All the dusts and washes in the world cannot be a substitute for good cultivation. It would be easy to complete a vast list of pests and diseases but the purpose of this chapter is simply to mention some of the commoner troubles and if the reader wishes to learn more about pests and diseases he should consult one of the standard works on the subject. Let us first consider some of the physiological disorders which are not caused by pests or diseases.

WATER PROBLEMS

The incorrect use or non-use of water to compost, foliage or atmosphere can cause serious disorders. Obviously the dry plant, if it is not at a resting period, will wilt but it is not always realised that a growing plant, if overwatered, will also wilt and may die. It is important to ensure that plants, particularly in the winter and when in plastic pots, are not over-watered. Some of the first signs of over-watering may be a yellowing of leaves followed by leaf fall, although this is not necessarily true. Over-watering may sometimes show as a brown rot on leaves which later may be attacked by disease. Hairy foliage such as that of Saintpaulia will show pale spots where water is allowed to drop on the foliage and in some tender-leaved plants serious scorching can result when water is applied to the foliage in strong sunlight. Flowers and flower buds of some plants, e.g. Azalia may drop off or fail to open if the atmosphere is not sufficiently humid and generally speaking pollination and fertilisation is poor under dry atmospheric conditions. The tomato under prolonged dry atmospheric conditions will not set well and we refer to it as dry set. Tomatoes may reach marble size and fail to develop further, assuming the flowers themselves did not drop off.

A common disorder of tomatoes is called blossom end rot. A sunken and blackened area develops at the blossom end of the swelling tomato fruit. Where this area is hard and not rotten it is considered to be caused by irregularities in the supply of water to the young fruit soon after it started swelling. Some tender seedlings when raised in humid conditions in early spring may show white blisters on leaves. This may be caused by the seedling being supplied with too much water which under humid conditions could not be transpired.

Draughts can cause serious leaf fall, particularly in Poinsettia and in Stephanotis. The Monstera, often grown in the dwelling-house, is another plant which dislikes a draught intensely. In the greenhouse if heating is by means of a fan heater it should be so sited that rapidly moving air does not blow directly on seedlings or tender leafed plants.

Some deficiencies of plant foods will result in quite characteristic disorders. A plant which requires acid soil conditions such as Azaleas if potted in a compost containing lime may show yellow leaves; and similar results may show if the level of potash is very high. Where the leaves yellow between the veins of the plant one should suspect magnesium deficiency and this can often be put right as in the case of tomatoes by the use of Epsom Salts, using one ounce dissolved in a gallon of water. If on the other hand the yellowing is at the growing point one might suspect iron deficiency and for this an iron salt such as Sequestrene can be used. Potash deficiency shows very markedly in tomatoes and fruits grown under glass as a brown marginal scorch to the leaves. It is also considered to be a cause of greenback of tomatoes.

Cultural inaccuracies will always bring problems. If one grows a plant in a temperature which is too low for it then one cannot expect it to succeed. The wrong variety of lettuce will not heart during short winter days and where plants require sunshine, if they are grown under shady conditions or overcrowded conditions, they must be expected to be thin and weedy.

Next let us consider some of the pests and diseases most likely to cause trouble in your greenhouse and frames and under cloches. It is not within the scope of this book to detail every pest and disease which could attack all the plants we discuss and much must be left to your detective ability.

ANTS

These are liable to infest the soil in pots, in frames and under cloches and they may affect aeration and drainage. They are also responsible for the movement of some greenfly as they appreciate the honey dew secreted by aphis.

CONTROL

In pots they can be removed by completely immersing in water. Ant powders containing B.H.C. can be dusted on the staging and outdoors nests should be found and destroyed.

APHIDES

Generally referred to as greenfly of which there are some thirty odd species in the country. They will attack most plants and increase at an amazing rate. Overwintering can be in the form of eggs which hatch in early spring but under glass active greenfly may be with us all the year round. Damage is noted as curling of the growing points often with malformation and colonies may be found clustered around young shoots and flowers. They feed by sucking the sap so permanent scars may often be left. The honey dew secreted by aphis forms a medium in which sooty moulds thrive and so a plant infected with aphis will often show sooty leaves.

Control. Aphis can be controlled with derris, with Malathion or by the use of a systematic insecticide containing Rogor. This material should not be used on chrysanthemums.

CATERPILLARS

These are larva of butterflies or moths and it seems to be mainly the moths which trouble the gardener. Carnations are very susceptible to their attack as also are tomatoes and geraniums. Caterpillars, if not checked, can quickly ruin chrysanthemum flowers by biting the side of the flower bud. In frames the cutworm may be responsible for the sudden collapse of lettuce plants. The pest can often be found by excavating around a collapsed lettuce plant.

Control. Much can be done by hand picking, particularly at night if a torch is used. Derris or B.H.C. dust or sprays can be used.

EELWORM

These are nematodes invisible to the naked eye which may cause trouble, particularly to chrysanthemums and to ferns, begonia, gloxinia, etc. Infested leaves are blackened and eventually die. Crinkles and banded areas may appear in ferns. In chrysanthemums the damage starts from the lower leaves and the blackened area is defined by the veins.

Control. Badly affected plants should be burnt but control of eelworm in chrysanthemum stools can be affected by what is known as the warm water treatment. This consists of immersing the stool in warm water at 115°F. (46°C.) for five minutes. Ferns should be immersed in water at 122 to 125°F. (50 to 51°C.). They should be repotted in sterilised soil.

HOPPERS

Both frog and leaf hoppers may cause considerable damage. The frog hopper in its mass of frothy cuckoo spit may attack greenhouse plants standing outside and will sometimes come into the house. The greenhouse leaf hopper produces a mottling on the foliage showing as bleached areas. They can often be seen and will attack all sorts of plants in various stages of growth.

Control. Malathion or nicotine washes directed on the undersides of the leaves should control hoppers.

LEAF MINER

The larva of the leaf miner tunnels in leaf tissue of many plants, particularly chrysanthemum and cineraria, leaving the characteristic pale tunnels showing. The larva can be seen when the infected leaf is held up to light. Some control can be effected by squashing the creatures in the leaf. Nicotine, Malathion and B.H.C. can all be used against this pest.

MEALY BUG

These creatures feed by sucking and establish themselves in colonies on plants covered with a mealy material. They can be serious and are difficult to remove because of their covering. Older plants such as climbers and vines can often become badly infected.

Control. In the case of deciduous plants such as vines and fruit trees tar oil winter wash can be employed but with evergreens this is not possible. Hand painting the colonies with methylated spirit gives control and also nicotine and B.H.C. Systemic insecticides can also be used.

RED SPIDER MITE

This is a very serious pest and once established is not easy to eradicate. It is a tiny pale orange coloured creature which feeds by sucking, usually on the under surface of leaves. Fruit, beans, fuchsias and cucumbers are very liable to attack and the first signs you notice may be cessation of growth and sickly yellow leaves. The mites can just be seen feeding along the veins. This creature revels in hot dry conditions.

Control. The first line of attack must be the maintenance of a more humid atmosphere and if this is provided throughout the plant's growing season red spider will not normally establish itself. The use of Rogor is one of the most effective methods of control, although white oil is also effective.

SCALE INSECT

These are rather similar to mealy bug in that they do not move around when established but in this case they are covered with a brown scale-like covering.

Control. As for mealy bug.

THRIP

These insects can be a great nuisance in the greenhouse because they spread so quickly and can disfigure foliage and flowers with a quite characteristic silvery marking coupled with some distortion. They are only tiny creatures but can be seen with the naked eye although as they are only about 1/20 in. or so in length they have to be searched for. Most glasshouse plants may be attacked and you may find that similar markings and distortions appear on peas out-doors.

Control. In the greenhouse the maintenance of a more humid atmosphere and the syringing of under leaves will act as a deterrent and nicotine or B.H.C. used as a dust should keep it under control.

WHITE FLY

This small fly can easily be recognised because when disturbed it rises in white clouds. It may affect many greenhouse plants, in particular the tomato and cineraria. Sooty moulds may follow attack by white fly just as they do attacks by aphides.

Control. Malathion or B.H.C. should give control but it should be repeated in ten to fourteen days.

WOODLICE

These small bugs which curl into a ball may feed on young plant material and live in dark corners and decaying wood in the green-house.

Control. Trapping in hollowed out potatoes, hygiene and the use of wireworm dust or naphthalene should keep them away.

VINE WEEVIL

This is often a pest particularly in older houses where hygiene is not sufficiently practised. The first signs may be the collapse of a cyclamen plant and on examination you find several $\frac{1}{2}$ in. long pale grubs are feeding on the roots at the base of the corm. The adult is brown to black in colour, $\frac{1}{2}$ in. long and with a pair of very pro-nounced and elbowed antennae. The adult is nocturnal and an old remedy used to be to spread a sheet on the ground under the vine and to give the vine rods a smart tap. This dislodged the creature which could be gathered from the sheet. Adult weevils mainly affect foliage and you may find a similar creature sitting on the edge of the pea or bean leaf under cloches and digging out chunks from the leaf edge.

Control. B.H.C. has been used watered in the compost with cycla-men and as a spray outside.

ALGAE

This green scum can be unsightly and it may effect aeration as it can cover soil, pots and staging.

Control. Zineb used as a spray in the early stages and regularly repeated should limit this trouble.

BOTRYTIS (Grey Mould)

This is a serious fungoid disease always present in the atmosphere and may establish itself on leaves, stems, fruit and flowers and any wounds are particularly liable to attack. The fungus is encouraged by humid still air and tomatoes, vines and fruits are very susceptible. It is often the cause of failure of lettuce under glass. The plants collapse and grey fungus spores are seen on the rotted leaves.

Control. Ample ventilation is important and care should be taken not to wet the leaves of lettuce under glass. Seedlings must never be overcrowded and any damaged plants or plant material should be removed and burnt. Captan as a dust or as a spray where leaves can safely be wetted is an effective control. Thiram and P.C.N.B. can also be used.

DAMPING OFF

There are several damping off and foot rot diseases which can affect young plants, particularly when raising seedlings. The seedling simply collapses and usually a brown collapsed area is present on the stem at about soil level.

Control. The use of sterilised seed and potting composts and the application of Cheshunt Compound should eliminate this trouble.

MILDEWS

There are two main forms of mildews which may attack your plants. Powdery mildew appears as a grey-white covering on the upper surface of leaves of chrysanthemums and of fruit and the mycelium threads may make a complete mat covering grapes. Downy mildew may be a serious disease of lettuce under glass and appears as a pale area on the upper leaf and a white or grey powdery area on the under side.

Control. Always give the plant its correct growing conditions and make sure there is plenty of air movement. Ventilate frames and cloches whenever possible. Powdery mildew can be controlled with Karathane or sulphur dusts and downy mildew is better controlled with copper sprays or Zineb.

TOMATO LEAF MOULD

This tomato disease appears under conditions of high humidity and poor ventilation. The upper surface of the leaves will show pale blotches and the undersides a greyish mould gradually turning to dark purple or brown. In some cases the blotches coalesce and the foliage is destroyed.

Control. Give as much ventilation as possible—if necessary remove a pane of glass to effect this. The use of copper sprays or Zineb is an effective control.

RUSTS

Rusts appear as small areas on leaf and stem which erupt sending out masses of spores. These are usually yellow or brown in colour, although with chrysanthemums there is a new rust called white rust where the eruptions are white in colour. If you have this the Ministry of Agriculture, Fisheries and Food should be notified. Carnations are very susceptible to carnation rust and it will seriously lower the vitality of the plant.

Control. The best control is zineb.

VIRUS DISEASES

These are diseases which are not fully understood and in some cases where the attack is mild seem to have little effect on the plant. Chrysanthemums are susceptible and an infected plant may be dwarfer than healthy plants and will usually have flowers with colour breaks or streaks in the petals. There are quite a few virus diseases which affect the tomato causing stunting, loss of vigour and sometimes malformation of leaves and growing point. Some common greenhouse plants may contain virus diseases which show as rings in the leaves but seem to do little other damage. There is no control for virus diseases and one can only suggest that where one is certain virus is present the plant be destroyed.

Index